# DEVELOPMENTAL CONTINUITY

## ACROSS
## PRESCHOOL
## AND
## PRIMARY
## GRADES

## Implications for Teachers

Nita H. Barbour, Associate Professor
University of Maryland-Baltimore County

Carol Seefeldt, Professor
University of Maryland at College Park

ASSOCIATION FOR CHILDHOOD EDUCATION INTERNATIONAL
11501 Georgia Ave., Suite 315, Wheaton, MD 20902
301-942-2443 • 800-423-3563

*Mary Renck Jalongo, Consulting Editor*
*Lucy Prete Martin, Director of Publications/Editor*
*Anne Watson Bauer, Assistant to Director of Publications/Production Editor*

**Photographs**
Cover & pages 6, 10, 30, 60, © 1993, Donna M. Leone
Page 74, © 1993, Robert Finken
Page 84, © 1993, Greg Vojtko Photography

---

*Library of Congress Cataloging-in-Publication Data*
Barbour, Nita.
    Developmental continuity across preschool and primary grades/
Nita H. Barbour and Carol Seefeldt.
        p.   cm.
    Includes bibliographical references.
    ISBN 0-87173-128-2
    1. Early childhood education—United States—Curricula.
    2. Articulation (Education)—United States.   I. Seefeldt, Carol.
    II. Title.
    LB1139.4.B37   1993
    372.19—dc20                                              93-599
                                                             CIP

---

# Contents

# Introduction

Claudia and Consuela, teachers at different schools in the same district, are having dinner together. Claudia exclaims,

**❝** What is this business of developmental continuity? Mr. B, my principal, came by and said that we're going to have someone from the central office come and talk to us about it."

"That's really interesting," replies Consuela. "Our school is going to be used as a pilot school for this developmental continuity. We began the process really because of our parents."

"Really," says Claudia, "tell me about it."

"Well, at a PTA meeting a couple of years ago an irate father asked just what we were doing to his son. It seems that he'd sent his son to the preschool program next door, where the child could choose his activities and where he loved 'reading' books, telling stories and 'writing' messages. Kindergarten, which followed, wasn't too bad, it seems, because the child could occasionally paint and make some choices after he completed his alphabet pages. The father's real frustration came after his son entered 1st grade—he was losing all interest and delight in school. The child had no choices and because he didn't do his alphabet pages, he was being made to feel he couldn't read. The father questioned whether 1st grade had to be so rigid. He was seeing his son go from loving books to a real dislike for reading."

"How did you respond to that?" asks Claudia.

"Of course, there were many different reactions and lots of dialogue, but eventually we began to realize that children ought not to have to adjust to major changes as they move from home to preschool to regular school experiences. It was then that we started to reach out to the teachers in our neighborhood preschool. We are sincere about changing our curriculum, so we can provide smoother transitions and continuity of curriculum for children from preschool through the primary grades. We are even including the child care director and some of the teachers in this planning."

"But do you think it is working?" asks Claudia.

"We're really enthusiastic about the changes we've made. Throughout this pilot year, we've spent a lot of time working with the teachers who had our kids last year and those who will have them next year. We are realizing how much more all of us can do with these kids when we know them better. At this point some of us are considering working with the same group over a longer period of time so we can provide the best and most interesting instruction."

"I can understand how knowing the kids better is helpful," challenges Claudia, "but how can you manage in a classroom of 35 kids to meet each child's needs and still have three reading groups! Because you have 'the top group,' your principal expects you to have most of your 1st-graders in 2nd- or 3rd-grade readers by the end of the year. Never mind that half of them are freaking out! How do you see developmental continuity figuring into that kind of thinking?"

"I'm not sure that the notion of three reading groups is very compatible with developmental continuity," replies Consuela. "Before we became involved in developmental continuity at my school, some of us had been trying to change our reading instruction to be more congruent with a whole language philosophy. Now, I'm finding that I think differently about how children learn to read. Not only has my classroom instruction become more flexible, but I'm learning more about each child's interests and learning processes. Really, I'm finding that I have more time for each individual child."

"How does that tie in with developmental continuity? Maybe if you gave me an example of what you do it would help."

"I'm not sure where to begin," replies Consuela, "because I find that I use so many different strategies. Remember how we used to think that the language experience approach to reading (LEA) was such a wonderful way to start the teaching of reading? Now I have a much broader concept of what that method was all about. Those who have supported and helped me understand whole language expanded my knowledge of LEA. What is really exciting for me now, however, is that I teach much more of an integrated curriculum and allow children to acquire concepts and develop needed skills at their own level of development."

"That still doesn't tell me what you do," persists Claudia.

"You are right," concedes Consuela. "In my 2nd-grade class, we discuss at least one 'topic' each day, and that topic can last several days. For example, last week we were involved in what animals make good pets and why. Children read a variety of materials about that topic, and then they wrote, drew and, in some graphic way, expressed what they got from their reading. Typically, we make all sorts of lists: concepts we have learned, new words we have discovered, rules for an area of the classroom, directions for making things. We read as a total group, usually poetry or some dramatic presentation. Children read to each other and to me, as well as silently. Writing is a way of life for both the children and me nowadays. Journals, books, lists are only the beginning. I find doing things this way allows me to work more with children individually and to be more knowledgeable about what their developmental needs are."

"How do you get away with not using the basals?" asks Claudia.

"Oh, I use the basals—when there are stories that are interesting and pertinent." Consuela continues, "The children are getting good at finding stories in the basals relating to the topics that interest them. They share a lot of the stories they like from those basal readers."

"You do sound excited about it," Claudia admits. "But I don't know if my principal would ever let me do something like that. He is so gung-ho about phonics."

"Make no mistake," says Consuela. "I teach plenty of phonics, but I teach those phonic skills children need as they are writing or trying to figure out a new word in their reading. And I didn't get there overnight. It took time and experimenting. Of course, I had a lot of support you may not have. My principal is very interested in having us all know more about developmental continuity, and she was the first one in the district to encourage us to go to workshops on whole language and to experiment with some of the techniques. She hired substitutes for me, so I could visit teachers who were succeeding with these techniques. When I began experimenting, these same teachers welcomed my questions and one even came to my classroom to observe me and give me some feedback. Another teacher in the school became involved when I did, and we've supported one another. The principal has made us feel that she has been learning along with us.

"Our principal does believe in keeping up with change," Consuela continues. "Because of changes in our neighborhood, the children in our school enter kindergarten with even more different educational experiences than in former years. Many have attended the Head Start program or the child care center in the neighborhood, but several have had no preschool experiences. And there are even a few children coming from the shelter for the homeless. The principal called the directors of the Head Start and child care programs and invited them to start working with us. First, the directors and principal just visited back and forth; then we began the tradition of bringing the children to visit the 'big school' before actual entrance; and now we all attend training sessions together. All of us are beginning to understand better what children at different stages need to learn in order to work productively together and to initiate their own learning.

"Claudia, you know, I could help you. Why don't you try it? We've always tried to support one another. Try some of the ideas this year, and I'll help you," encourages Consuela.

"Gee, I don't know. Maybe I could try. I should ask my principal if he'd support me if I tried some of these ideas. You know, I could start small maybe—by expanding the language experience approach as you did. I have used that technique and I really did enjoy it, before I got so pressured into using only basals. Do you really think," Claudia queries, "that I could be as successful as you have been? **99**

Can Claudia be successful in implementing curriculum that responds to children's developmental progress?

It depends.

Claudia's success depends, in part, on her own commitment to developing educational experiences that match children's development, and in part on the support she receives from the school system and her administrators. Even if Claudia is successful, the continued success of children will depend on something else—whether or not all of their teachers across the preschool and primary grades can work together to create continuity in children's early educational experiences.

This book, *Developmental Continuity Across Preschool and Primary Grades: Implications for Teachers*, is a resource for teachers as they work together to provide experiences that respond to children's developmental progress from preschool through primary grades.

Chapter 1 discusses the meaning of developmental continuity and its history; Chapter 2 offers suggestions for beginning the change process. Because developmental continuity is difficult without changes in the organization of schools and coordination among preschool, kindergarten and primary grades, changes in the structure of schools are necessary. The requisite changes are described in Chapter 3. Chapter 4 revolves around the creation of a curriculum that responds to children's development, while Chapter 5 gives suggestions for structuring the environment in which that curriculum will be implemented. Finally, Chapter 6 deals with evaluation issues and discusses methods for documenting children's progress and achievement. Together, these six chapters provide readers with an action plan for putting the principles of developmental continuity into practice.

# CHAPTER 1

# Developmental Continuity: Its Meaning

**&#x275D;** You talked about developmental continuity, whole language and integrated curriculum while you described what you have been doing to provide for the kids' developmental progress," persists Claudia when she and her friend meet later. "But, just what does developmental continuity mean? **&#x275E;**

Developmental continuity is a term used to describe a way of designing early childhood instruction. Curriculum is designed to provide learning experiences that are linked to children's prior knowledge, that flow in a natural progression across the preschool and primary grades toward more sophisticated and complex content, and that permit progress according to each child's rate and style of learning. As children acquire knowledge, learn skills and develop positive attitudes toward learning, new experiences provide increasingly sophisticated, abstract and complex practices.

There are different ways of providing for developmental continuity. Common to all methods is the idea that teachers, parents and administrators work together to provide a continuum of developmentally appropriate educational experiences for children.

Providing developmentally appropriate experiences involves:
- basing curriculum and education decisions on each child's social, emotional, physical and intellectual development
- adjusting teaching and schooling so all children experience success and demonstrate progress in academic achievement appropriate to their individual learning styles.

Teachers, parents and administrators across the preschool and primary grades work together to provide developmental continuity by:
- eliminating artificial barriers, such as grade or group placement according to achievement tests, that negate continuity of achievement and progress as children move from the preschool to the kindergarten and through the primary grades
- planning curriculum that provides a spiral of knowledge, skills and experiences from preschool through the primary grades
- ensuring smooth transitions for children as they move from the preschool to kindergarten and primary grades.

## DEVELOPMENT IS CONTINUOUS

Children's development is continuous, sequential and hierarchical. While children's social, emotional, physical or cognitive growth and development may be uneven, with one area of development spurting ahead of another, different areas of children's development cannot be viewed separately. Their "mental growth is inseparable from physical growth," and "it is widely accepted that cognitive and affective or social development are inseparable and parallel" (Piaget & Inhelder, 1969, p. vii, p. 117).

Just as children's development is continuous, so is their learning. The research of Jean Piaget, which forever changed our thinking of how children think and learn, clearly illustrated that children's thinking and learning are the result of different stages of development and that certain kinds of learning depend upon both the level of maturation and the child's experiences with the social, physical and intellectual environments.

For the first two years of life, children learn through sensorimotor experiences that enable them to form beginning concepts and language about their immediate environment. A young child feels, touches and often even tastes objects that are new to her. She may attempt to pick up a bean. If unsuccessful, she may proceed to squash it and get a piece of it on her fingers in the process. Then she may put the piece in her mouth and say, "Bee, mmm" in imitation of her mother's description, "It's a bean and it's yummy."

During the next seven years, from age 2 through about age 8, children are in the preoperational period of thinking. Children's thinking at the preoperational stage is characterized by their excessive reliance on perception instead of logic. Evidence of children's reliance on perception is seen in Piaget's conservation experiments, where he witnessed children's inability to recognize the stability of an amount of a liquid or a solid when the container for the liquid or form of the solid was changed. It takes lots of experiences before children realize that there is the same amount of cereal in a high narrow bowl as there is in a low wide bowl even when the cereal is poured from one bowl to another. Logic and experience inform the more sophisticated thinker that the amounts are the same, but for the preoperational child who is bound by her perceptions, the high narrow bowl has more cereal (or the low wide bowl, depending on her perception of "biggest").

At the same time, children are growing in ability to use symbols and imagery. This ability is reflected in the rapid growth of language. From using words for immediate things or actions, to using language as beginning steps in reasoning, children progress to learning increasingly abstract forms of language—writing and reading.

Nevertheless, whether children are 4, 5, 6 or 7 years old, their thinking is bound to the real world. They do not yet have the intellectual freedom to make possible the contemplation of the hypothetical, to compare the ideal with the actual, or to be concerned about the discrepancy between this world and that which they imagine possible (Lefrancois, 1989). The young child, bound to his experiences yet impatient to get to Gramma's, wishes the red light to change to green. When it does, he is convinced that his wishing caused the light to change. Reality for him is what he perceives is happening.

Even after 7 or 8, when children are able to perform mental operations, their thought is still bound to the real world. For many children, thinking requires that concrete objects, people, things or events be present. For example, children at this age can determine their classmates' height: if Mary is taller than Bill and Bill is taller than Joe, then Mary must be taller than Joe. They can see the reality of the situation and thus reason logically. It will not be until 11 or 12 years of age that children are able to think and reason abstractly—whereby they could solve the abstract problem: which is the farthest away, given that the library is farther than the fire station and the fire station is farther than the community hall? Such hypothetical reasoning without the reliance on real objects requires abstract thinking.

Because children's learning throughout the period of early childhood is governed by their preoperational thinking, whether in a preschool, kindergarten or primary classroom, children learn through:
- interactions as a result of their own social, mental and physical activity
- continuity of integrated experiences
- using language in conjunction with reflection.

## Interactions

During the preoperational period of growth, from age 2 to about 7 or 8, all children need to be mentally, socially and physically active in order to learn. When activity centers are arranged throughout the preschool and primary rooms—with spaces for building, art, music, reading, board game play, dramatic play, writing, math and science, and time to use these spaces and materials—children have the opportunity to learn through firsthand physical activity.

As children work in centers of interest, they are able to relate with one another. They comment on each other's work, spontaneously offering criticism and information as they exchange ideas and prior knowledge in a cooperative effort. The necessity to compromise, to adjust their thinking to take into account the ideas of others, is real and invaluable for children's social, emotional and intellectual growth. Vygotsky (1986) believed that this type of social activity was needed as the generator of thought. He believed that individual consciousness is built from outside through relations with others. "The mechanism of social behavior and the mechanism of consciousness are the same" (Vygotsky, 1986, p. ii).

## Continuity of Experiences

Because children's growth is continuous from preschool through the primary grades, they require educational experiences that are equally continuous. Stated simply, this means that throughout the period of early childhood, one learning experience will build on another. A thread of meaning runs through a number of experiences. Experiences, activities and lessons are juxtaposed to enable children to see connections between the past and the present, among and between people and the objects and events of their world.

For example, 2nd-graders' interest in a stray kitten led to reading a story about cats and kittens, which led to reading reference books about cats and kittens. Sizes and weights of cats were graphed. After a trip to the zoo to observe large cats, the children created a class mural of cats living in the wild, in zoos and in homes. A veterinarian visited the class, bringing with her a cat skeleton. Comparisons between cat and human bones were made. These experiences, presented as a continuous whole, gave the children an opportunity to develop conceptual relationships among the separate subjects of physiology, mathematics, language and science (Eisner, 1988).

Continuity of experiences also means that curriculum from the preschool across the primary grades will be coordinated and continuous. As 2nd-grade children go to the zoo for the primary purpose of observing the large cats, the experiences and remembrances of previous visits during the preschool years should be recorded and links made to the new trip and purpose.

Experiences developed for skill-building need continuity. Before children will be able to write in 1st and 2nd grade, they need opportunities with scribbling and drawing in preschool and kindergarten, as well as observing their own words written down and experimenting with writing sounds as they hear them. Children cannot be asked to direct their own learning in the primary grades without a background of initiating their own learning during their preschool and kindergarten experiences. Children need time and opportunity to develop the skills involved in being self-directing, making plans, setting their own goals and finding ways to achieve these goals.

### Covered with Language

Children learn through activity centers because these centers make the need for language real and necessary. "Children not only speak about what they are doing, their speech and action are part of one and the same complex psychological function" (Vygotsky, 1986). While talking, arguing, discussing, listening, reading and writing, children clarify their experiences.

Children converse informally as they work together on a puzzle, rotate eggs in an incubator or construct a space station. They talk about what they are doing or tell about what happened yesterday or continue an argument that occurred on the playground. Allowing this type of talk in the classroom gives children the chance to practice their skills in explaining, clarifying, making points and arguing over events; it "contributes substantially to intellectual development in general, and literacy growth in particular" (Dyson, 1987, p. 397).

Teachers' language is important as well. They intervene, model, question and help children develop other ways of discussing or arguing. Tillie, a 1st-grader, became upset when her friend Mary said accusingly, "You told Aletha you didn't like me." "No! I didn't," Tillie argued. "Uh, huh, yes you did!" Mary argued back. After a few moments of this dialogue, Tillie complained to the teacher. The teacher asked, "Did you ask what Aletha *really* said?" When Tillie posed that question to Mary, she said, "Aletha said you didn't like me when I copied your picture." "Well, I didn't," responded Tillie, "but I like you now that we're drawing our own pets." "Yeah, it's more fun," replied a pleased Mary.

In addition to informal exchanges like these, formal discussions take place and are equally important. Both large group and small group formal discussions provide opportunities for children's growth and learning. When formal classroom discourse is the only mode of conversation, however, there can be problems. Research suggests that during these discussions teacher talk dominates, teachers select topics, and there is a pattern of teacher-question-child-response dialogue. If formal discussions are used exclusively, this leaves few opportunities for children to initiate ideas, argue points, listen to other children's responses or follow another's argument (Cazden, 1986; Cook, Gumperz & Gumperz, 1982; Flanders, 1970; Morine-Dershimer & Tenenberg, 1992).

By thoughtfully planning large group discussions, however, teachers can help children grow in their ability to follow an idea, argue a point and listen to others' viewpoints. Follow-up in small group discussions can provide the practice for appropriate group interactions. These follow-up sessions should be both planned and spontaneous. It is during the spontaneous sessions that teachers will gain insights into children's achievements.

### Reflection

Learning requires reflection. Throughout the preschool and primary grades, children need to be able to think about what they have done and to reflect on their actions and ideas if they are to learn. They should be encouraged to: 1) organize their ideas and experiences, 2) communicate and present their findings to others, 3) apply what they have learned and 4) evaluate their work.

*1. Organizing Their Own Ideas and Experiences.* Children can organize their ideas by drawing a picture, writing a story, making a graph or chart, constructing a bulletin or creating a display. As children engage in these experiences, the skilled teacher observes and offers suggestions when appropriate to help children organize their experiences. For a child who quickly draws one object and is "done," the teacher might engage the child in recalling events that led to her selecting this picture to draw. Children writing stories might be able to extend their own story if the teacher assists them in recalling the sequence of events. Before making individual graphs or charts, children need to participate in making group graphs or charts of classroom events.

In one classroom, a teacher had stickers of different fruits. As children selected the fruit they liked best, they placed their stickers in the appropriate column on the prepared graph paper. Children could then tell which fruit was most popular. By laminating a graph, many different preferences could be checked out as children's skills in graphing developed.

In a 1st-grade classroom, children charted the monthly weather by placing a picture representing the particular weather on a homemade calendar. At the end of the month, the children could determine the number of rainy days, sunny days, cloudy days, etc. They also could determine which of the weekdays had the best weather overall for the month.

*2. Communicating and Presenting Their Findings to Others.* Even 4- and 5-year-olds can be asked to communicate their ideas and work to others. Rather than always asking preschool children to share during the morning opening group time, it is useful to invite children to share after their work time. Then children can tell the group how they made something or what they accomplished during work time. This gives them the opportunity not only to organize their ideas and experiences, but also to communicate and present these to others. Some children seem to grow into this ability naturally. For others, the skill needs to be nurtured.

One kindergarten teacher who regularly used this technique found that one of her 5-year-olds always forgot what he wanted to share at the end of the day. She began to remind him during work time that he would be asked to share what he was doing. Then she would briefly rehearse his activity with him in private. Initially she would ask him to tell what he did first to make his plane and what his next step was. As he became able to tell these two things during the class session without prompting, she then asked for more elaborate steps. Gradually he became skilled at sharing without her assistance.

*3. Applying What They Have Learned.* As new projects or topics are begun, both teacher and children reflect on what they have learned and how they can apply the new knowledge or skill to a new task. Learning about land masses, 3rd-graders acquired the skill of segmenting words into parts, when they needed to figure out the word *peninsula*. As they learned how to segment one word, the children then began to use that skill to read unknown words in books. Children, who had previously learned how to measure the area of their sand table, applied and transformed those measuring skills to the task of figuring out how much material they needed to cover the floor of their playhouse.

*4. Evaluating Their Own Work.* Children should be asked to think about and evaluate their own progress and work both in informal and formal ways. Even 4- and 5-year-olds can be asked to make judgments about what they did and learned during the day. One 5-year-old in the block area figured out how to balance a particular block for his construction, after several trials. An astute teacher observed his efforts and asked him to share with the class how he had accomplished the task. Although he needed the blocks—the concrete materials—to accompany his evaluation of his accomplishment, he was able to tell the other children that it took "patience and I had to keep trying." Children in the primary grades can keep records of their stories and checklists of the skills they have learned, and compare their current work to that completed during the beginning of the school year. By so doing, children monitor their own learning, set their own goals, and experience the joy and satisfaction of accomplishing these goals.

## THE PROBLEM

It is no secret; today's schools are under great pressure. Everyone wants the best for children. No one wants a child to fail, or even to be below average. Under pressure to ensure that every child succeeds, educators have tried to gain more control over children's educational experiences. Children's success often has been interpreted to mean achieving a predetermined standard within a given grade. To achieve this end, many educators have adopted a behavioral approach. Curricula for different grade levels have been established with clearly stated behavioral objectives, performance standards or competencies that all children in a school system are expected to achieve within a given time frame.

When inflexible policies exist, education is treated like a timed test. Only those children who master age-grade content are permitted to enter school or move on to the next grade. Children are judged inadequate or unready for placement in the next group if they have not mastered the content.

In the past, scores on standardized achievement tests became the yardstick of success. Because they were thought to document success, test scores became more important than children. Curriculum was designed around the content of the test, not on the past experiences, needs, interests or developmental levels of the children. As a result of such standardization, in many schools today children's early experiences have become structured and teacher-centered. Children's play and activity have been limited. Teacher-directed learning activities, not play or child-centered activities, dominate the learning environment (Mitchell & Modigliani, 1989). Kindergarten and primary classes come to look and sound like any other classroom in the "eyes on me" traditional teacher-directed school (Karweit, 1988, p. 124). Instead of children learning by interacting with others and by observing and experimenting with how things work, they are expected to learn by sitting still, listening and following instructions.

When curriculum is designed to teach children a set of abstract and isolated academic skills within a given time frame, young children still in the preoperational stage of thinking will have difficulty. Unable to make sense of isolated and abstract content, and denied the opportunity to learn through their own physical, mental and social activity, children often fail. In fact, in many areas of the United States nearly 49 percent of all children will fail, or be retained in grade, by the time they reach the 3rd grade (Walsh, 1989).

From the way many schools operate today, one is reminded of the Greek myth of Procrustes, referred to by Goodlad and Anderson (1959) in their book *The Nongraded Elementary School*. When travelers sought Procrustes' house for shelter, he tied them to an iron bedstead. If the traveler were shorter than the bed, Procrustes stretched the person to the same length as the bed. If the person were longer, limbs were chopped off so the person could fit the bed. Procrustes shaped both short and tall until they were equally long and dead.

Developmental continuity is jeopardized when children are forced by Procrustes-like methods to fit the system instead of adapting the system to fit the child. Children entering kindergarten with a background of learning in child-centered, play-oriented programs find the early academic demands of kindergarten confusing, stressful and sometimes impossible to achieve. To accommodate these children, as well as those who do not seem "ready" for the structured, rigid curriculum, schools have implemented a number of policies. Some screen children on a variety of measures and systematically exclude from educational programs those deemed "unready." Others have raised the entrance age so only older children, those who have a better chance developmentally of achieving the fixed curriculum, will be in school. In both cases, the child is required to be "ready" to change to fit the school. But whom are the schools for? And whose interests are being served by such policies?

Ultimately, inflexible public policies have a "trickle down" effect on the child care, nursery and preschool community. Desperate to prepare children for kindergarten and the primary grades, preschools are becoming more academic. Thinking that earlier introduction to isolated academic skills will better prepare children for the rigors of the accelerated academic kindergarten and primary grades, many preschools limit children's play and active learning in favor of learning the alphabet in a pre-scribed, sequential and isolated fashion.

Even when children's preschool experiences respond to their developmental progress, there can be problems later. Children used to learning through play and activity, encouraged to make decisions and gain autonomy, find adjustment to academic kindergarten difficult. The continuity of learning so necessary throughout the early years is disrupted as children move from the preschool to a very different educational experience found in the elementary school. Intellectual curiosity, excitement for learning, important thinking skills, concepts and knowledge about one's own world can be sadly thwarted by rigid curricula that require children to learn isolated skills and facts.

Given this situation, there is a sense of urgency to provide developmental continuity across the preschool and primary years. The premise is that if the curriculum throughout the preschool and primary grades continually responded "to the learning patterns of children within a given age range, to individual differences among children, and to cultural and linguistic diversity among children" (National Association of State Boards of Education, 1988, p. 1), then so many children would not fail. The end result promises that larger numbers of children will find school a place where they can achieve, find respect and continue to grow—not a place where children become failures if they do not measure up to artificial standards in a narrowly designated time period.

## CONTINUITY ACROSS THE YEARS

Concern for developmental continuity across the preschool and primary grades is not new. It may have started with the establishment of the first kindergarten programs in the late 1880s. The first kindergartens, probably much like today's child care centers or preschools, were operated by philanthropists, churches or other civic and charitable organizations.

A great deal of emphasis on social services and family support was evident. The kindergartners, as the teachers were called, "prided themselves on their ability to establish relationships with families and to perform socially beneficial tasks" (Beatty,

1989, p. 77). The curriculum in these first kindergartens, which revolved around Froebel's gifts and occupations, was one of play and activity. Play has long been recognized as important for young children's growth. As two early childhood educators expressed it: "The plays of this age are the heart-leaves of the whole future life; for the whole man is visible in them, in his finest capacity, in his innermost being" (Wiggan & Smith, 1896, p. 146).

Because of their popularity, the first kindergartens soon became a part of the public school system. But after programs for 5-year-olds were housed in public schools, changes occurred. The kindergarten teachers found little time for home visits or community work and instead of being able to follow the traditional Froebelian curriculum of play, they were pressured to get children ready for 1st grade.

Conflict ensued. The kindergarten teachers who wanted to "bring more enjoyment and more socializing experiences into children's lives" (Parker & Temple, 1925, p. 2) resisted integration with primary grades. On the other hand, primary teachers found fault with the "kindergartners" (kindergarten teachers). They believed "kindergartners failed to recognize the importance of the essential social skills in reading, writing, and arithmetic, which the primary school historically has emphasized in response to defined social needs" (p. 2).

Attempting to bring more continuity between kindergarten and 1st grade, Samuel Parker and Alice Temple wrote *Unified Kindergarten and First-Grade Teaching* in 1925. They believed that because children's mental abilities were the same from kindergarten through 1st grade, there should be no break between the two in curriculum methods. Rather, kindergarten and 1st-grade curricula should be "continuous and delightful" (Parker & Temple, 1925, p. 1).

On the one hand, "play and games, construction and drawing, and the study of social life and nature, which were once considered the peculiar curriculum of the kindergarten, now continue through the first grade" (Parker & Temple, 1925, p. 1). On the other hand, Parker and Temple advocated the introduction of skills, reading readiness and other school content into the kindergarten. If the gap between kindergarten and 1st grade was really to be eliminated, then reading instruction should be introduced to kindergarten children whose mental ages would "assure successful learning of this useful art" (p. 1).

### Nongraded Units

Efforts to make children's education continuous throughout the early years didn't end with Parker and Temple. During the 1940s and early 1950s, nongraded primary units were created as a "way of adjusting teaching and administrative procedures to meet the differing social, mental, and physical capacities among children" (Milwaukee Public Schools, 1942, p. 3).

Nongraded primary units weren't conceived as a method of teaching, "[or] a departure from established procedures long used by good teachers, but rather an administrative tool to encourage and promote a philosophy of continuous growth" (MPS, 1942, p. 3). Instead of making the child fit into the administrative system of the schools, nongraded units were designed to make the administrative system fit the nature of the child. Each child progressed at his/her own level in these primary units. Progress, whether fast or slow, was observed and recorded, and teaching was adjusted to the needs of each individual child. Teachers, once free from artificial restraint of grade placement, or the "blockings, frustrations, confusions, which often

18

develop under the scheme of grade barriers, artificial standards and traditional markings," were believed free to adjust their teaching to the child's developmental needs (MPS, 1942, p. 3).

A number of basal reading series, mathematics, science and social studies texts were available in each school. These were categorized by level and shared among teachers. With this abundance of materials, theoretically, every child's level of maturation could be matched to appropriate materials.

No child was ever asked to repeat what he/she had already learned. Each was provided with proper challenge and interests. Children needing more time were given it. High achieving children were given a "program of acceleration planned as carefully as that of the child who is growing slowly" (MPS, 1942, p. 4).

This individualized instruction and unity of program from kindergarten through grade 3 was believed able to eliminate the "piling up of problems at the end of the primary school period" (MPS, 1942, p. 4). Those who needed more time to move onto 4th-grade work would be few, but the needs of these children would be "handled skillfully and carefully" (MPS, 1942, p. 4).

Some say that these years of the nongraded primary unit were the kindest and fairest of all (Connell, 1987). But the units had problems. Evaluation was weak. Teachers alone were given the complex task of judging each child's progress and achievement. With no standardized form, reporting this progress was problematic. Parents often misunderstood the intent of the program. Without grades and grade placement, they were often very vocal about their need to know exactly what grade their children were in and to which grade they would be promoted in the following year.

In truth, well-developed nongraded kindergarten and primary units were the exception, not the rule. Goodlad and Anderson (1959) list fewer than 50 known operational units across the United States. Even in Milwaukee, believed to be one of the strongest examples of a nongraded primary unit, the strength of the program depended upon the individual school. In some schools, the principal, teachers and parents worked together as a team to create smoothly functioning, successful nongraded units; in many other schools, however, grade placement went on as usual.

Nor did these units last very long. In 1957, the Soviets blasted the first human-made satellite—Sputnik—into outer space. The race was on! Public pressure for achievement, especially of scientific knowledge that would put American children ahead of those in Russia, Germany or any other nation, was intense.

Educators responded with equal intensity. Many, in order to document children's achievement, focused the curriculum on isolated academic skills that they could show the children had, or had not, achieved within a given time frame. Content, perhaps appropriate for children in the 4th or 5th grade, was moved down to the 2nd or 3rd, so children would have to work harder and be better able to take their place among the successful scientists of the world. Under this intensity, the peaceful, kind and fair nongraded units of the 1940s and 1950s (with the exception of one or two units in California) disappeared.

### Concern Continued
Concern for developmental continuity did not disappear along with the nongraded units, however. In the late 1960s, concern for continuity between the preschool and elementary school led to new programs. Research indicating that Head Start children's

achievement gains dissipated by the end of kindergarten or 1st grade led the Office of Education to fund Project Follow Through. Designed to provide greater continuity of curriculum and teacher training from Head Start through grade 3, Follow Through projects were implemented in 37 communities. Model curricula were developed and presented to representatives from these communities, who selected a model that would be implemented across Head Start and the elementary grades.

Similar concerns led to the funding of Project Developmental Continuity (PDC) by the U.S. Department of Education in 1974. A national Head Start demonstration program, PDC was designed to promote continuity of curriculum and comprehensive child development services for children as they made the transition from Head Start to school. The project was based on the assumption that children's continuous and gradual growth and learning are enhanced when educational programs are planned according to each child's needs and flow out of previous experiences in the home and school.

But as it turned out, neither Project Follow Through nor Project Developmental Continuity was found to be totally effective in promoting continuity of children's early educational experiences. Each was found to be related to positive gains for some children in some communities and settings, but no program was found to completely fulfill its stated purposes (Berrueta-Clement, 1980; Krulee, Hetzner & McHenry, 1973; Seefeldt & Barbour, 1990; Stallings & Kaskowitz, 1974). It appears impossible to design a curriculum model, even if selected by community representatives, which can then be implemented with equally successful results for all children in that community.

Effective curriculum cannot be imposed on children. It may be that in the communities in which Follow Through and Developmental Continuity were effective, the curriculum model selected did, in fact, match children's interests and needs. Congruent with children's experiences in their home, school and community, these models, in specific settings, may have held meaning for children. Or it may be that the teachers in these communities were able to transcend the constraints of a programmed model and individualize the curriculum for each group of children and each child.

Curriculum innovators have continued to design programs with the intent of making children's education responsive to their developmental level. Ideas related to team teaching, open-space classrooms, open education, programs of discovery learning and cooperative learning are attempts to improve education for American children. All programs have had some modicum of success. Often, however, teachers were not involved in planning the innovations or were poorly prepared to implement the ideas in ways that responded to the needs, interests and developmental levels of all children. Large class sizes, the changing complexity of American society and the overwhelming problems some children bring into the schools put great stresses on the classroom teacher. Yet, the situation demands that the schools' success in educating every child according to his/her ability is vital if American society is to continue its leadership into the 21st century.

# CHAPTER 2

# Toward Developmental Continuity: Getting Started

**"** How did it all get started in the system?" Claudia asks in another session. "Well," answers Consuela, "it is difficult to tell where it all started, but I think that a kindergarten teacher and a 1st-grade teacher approached their principal to suggest redesigning their classrooms so that children in their rooms could have a more continuous flow of instruction. Both teachers had several parents who worked in their classrooms, so they enlisted these parents in the planning process. What exists now is the result of evolution that continues as we learn more about our successes and failures. **"**

Providing children with a continuum of educational experiences that respond to their development across the preschool and primary grades can begin with a single teacher or a group of teachers and a single classroom or unit. Actually, anyone or any one group can make the decision to work to provide continuity in children's learning, school programs and the classroom curriculum. Change can begin at the grassroots level, with a teacher or two or a principal or a group of parents taking leadership. Or change might be initiated at the administrative level, by the school board, superintendent or other school supervisor. Regardless of who initiates the project, the support and cooperation of the larger community, parents, preschool and child care workers, plus the business community will be necessary.

Change will take different evolutionary forms, depending on the nature of the program, the school community and other people involved. Projects and programs can be informal, even spontaneous, or they can be structured and systematized. Some programs are simple, others highly complex.

A project can be as easy, yet as useful, as creating a paper form to record children's progress from preschool through the primary grades. Or it can be as informal as a group of 1st- and 2nd-grade teachers within a school deciding to work together to create a curriculum that continues from one grade to the next. Simple projects and programs can lead to such major system-wide changes as restructuring kindergarten/primary units or replacing standardized testing with developmentally appropriate assessment methods.

## PROJECTS AIMED AT CONTINUITY

The following programs illustrate ways to provide developmental continuity. Some are simple ideas, easily implemented; others are more complex. Projects include nationally organized efforts and state or regional projects, as well as locally implemented ideas.

### National Projects
■ The Administration for Children, Youth and Families of the Department of Health and Human Services (1988) developed a multimedia kit, *Easing the Transition:*

*From Preschool to Kindergarten. A Guide for Early Childhood Teachers and Administrators*, based on Bronfenbrenner's (1979) thesis that transitions from one setting to another can be structured to enhance human potential. This program offers parents, teachers and administrators suggestions for promoting continuity from children's preschool experience to that of the kindergarten.

■ *Right from the Start*, by the National Association of State Boards of Education (1988), recommends a number of ways to create continuity of children's early educational experiences. Guidelines for school boards, parents and teachers who seek to create continuity of children's early educational experiences are given.

■ To enable Head Start children to maintain gains through the primary grades, the Administration for Children, Youth and Families has initiated the Head Start Transition Project. The project's purpose is to develop successful strategies where Head Start programs, parents, local education agencies and other community agencies can join together, plan and implement a coordinated and continuous program of comprehensive services, beginning in Head Start and continuing through kindergarten and the first 3 grades of public school.

### State and Regional Projects

■ The State of Missouri has developed *Project Construct*, implementing Piagetian-based curriculum in preschools, kindergartens and the primary grades. Teacher training, materials and support for schools changing from teacher-centered curriculum to Piagetian-based curriculum are provided.

■ The St. Louis Association for the Education of Young Children and the Southwestern Association for the Education of Young Children (1989) developed an *Early Childhood Transfer Form* to provide information about individuals and their prior experiences, in an attempt to promote continuity across the children's preschool and primary school experiences.

■ In New Jersey, the State Department of Education, Division of School Programs, Bureau of Curriculum (1989), developed a *Guide for Teachers, Administrators, Parents, and Parent Coordinators: Planning for Parental Involvement in Early Childhood Education*. The guide suggests many ways parents can work with schools and become involved in promoting education that responds to children's developmental level.

### Local Projects

■ Ann Martin, a kindergarten teacher in Brookline, Massachusetts, went before the school board and got permission to use narrative observations as a means of reporting to parents, instead of the system report card based on whether or not a child had achieved a specific competency (Martin, 1985). The school board, impressed with the documentation the teacher provided, reconsidered its policy and later accepted alternative forms of evaluating children.

■ In Washington, DC, the Office of Early Education in the District of Columbia Public Schools joined forces with the National Day Care Association, a Head Start grantee, and Teaching Strategies, Inc., a private materials development and training firm, in a three-year effort to promote continuity of children's early educational experiences. Strategies to ease children's transition from Head Start to the public schools were implemented, and training for teachers and parents in developmentally appropriate curriculum across the preschool and primary grades was conducted.

■ A principal of a Boston school created a mini-nongraded unit. Time was given for kindergarten, 1st- and 2nd-grade teachers to meet and plan the program together. Materials were collected that could be used by all children in any group. Reporting procedures were changed to respond to children's continuing progress.

■ In another school, kindergarten and 1st-grade teachers met together and agreed to accept each child's maturational level. They made plans to adapt their instruction to children, instead of the published curriculum. In this school, the changes began with just one kindergarten and one 1st-grade teacher, who met together during the summer to plan a curriculum that would begin in kindergarten and continue through 1st grade. Throughout the year, the two teachers met together to discuss the progress of individual children and the total group. At the end of the school year, they met again. The kindergarten teacher reviewed the progress of each child and the experiences of the total group. Based on this information, they made plans for the beginning of grade 1. Because the two teachers were successful, other teachers in the school organized team meetings; by the third year, all teachers at every grade level were planning together to meet children's developmental levels.

## PRINCIPLES OF PLANNING

Developing continuity can begin with a simple plan or a complex one. Successful programs depend, however, on committed people who are willing to find out about other successful programs, define what they are attempting, become skilled in communicating their ideas to others, eventually involve others, receive authorization for implementing their plans and, after succeeding in a small way, make plans for expanding the program. During the many phases of implementation, parents and the community need to be aware of the steps being taken and the progress of the children. Any committed person can initiate the process, but without committing others to the plan there will be only minimal success.

### Commitment

Regardless of the types of programs, whether there are changes in classroom practice, curriculum or school structure, commitment is necessary. Without commitment based on knowledge and understanding, the best of plans and intentions will fail. Open-space classrooms, built in such abundance during the 1970s, were intended to provide curriculum that would match children's needs for active learning with others. Far too many classrooms were designed, however, with the expectation that teachers, principals and parents would automatically understand the concept and initiate change. Although there were many successes, all too many teachers found open space disconcerting; today these classrooms are now divided into separate classrooms using partitions to define smaller spaces within one larger space.

The teacher who wants to begin changing the curriculum and school will need to find someone with whom to work. Shepard and Smith (1988) suggest that although a single teacher can change programs and curriculum within a school system, it is more realistic for a group of teachers to work together. They recommend that teachers wanting to make change toward developmental continuity join forces with a colleague or two. Working with someone else provides a support system and supplies feedback on one's ideas—successes as well as failures.

Teachers who seek change generally benefit from partnerships with colleagues, but they also need to recognize that change is a gradual, evolutionary process, not a revolutionary one. Teachers in the British Infant Schools were successful because they recognized this. When one U.K. teacher was asked how she managed to create such exemplary programs that continually responded to children's development, she replied: "You Americans! You're always so eager for a revolution, when what you need is evolution. We didn't just change from a rigid, authoritarian program overnight—we evolved our programs. It took time for us to evolve our philosophy, our ideas, and even more time for parents and others to evolve. But taking time was necessary for our Head Mistresses and Masters, the parents and our entire system, to unite in their commitment to making changes that would last."

### Finding Out
A good way to begin is to find out more about developmental continuity across the preschool and primary grades. Teachers might begin by reading everything they can about developmental continuity and finding someone with whom to discuss the ideas. An examination of the research and theory of developmental continuity and programs of the past not only will increase their understanding of continuity, but will give them insights into how to design, plan and implement their own program.

Next, a number of ongoing successful programs could be visited and observed. Goodlad and Anderson (1959) found that when leaders in school systems across the nation wanted to implement nongraded kindergarten/primary units during the 1950s, visits to successfully operating programs served a number of purposes. They found that visits were often more beneficial for psychological support than for collecting facts. Nongraded programs, or any other program of developmental continuity, look so normal in practice, they wrote, that any anxieties about changing current practice or programs were replaced with the assurance of normality.

### Defining
In reading about and observing programs, teachers will discover diverse ways of starting to change practices within their school and community. Examples of what they can use include the following:

■ In one school, the kindergarten and 1st-grade teachers decided to start reporting to parents, using narrative descriptions of children's growth to supplement the standard report card.

■ An Association for Childhood Education International group created a reporting form for children to take with them from their individual preschool experiences to the elementary school.

■ A group of 1st-grade teachers took a workshop on art as a means of early symbolization. They discovered that some children having difficulty with the structured reading and writing program were able to express their ideas and feelings by painting.

■ A school board designed and implemented a multi-age program from the 5-year-old kindergarten through 2nd grade.

■ In another community, child care teachers arranged for their children to visit the "big" school before their entrance into kindergarten.

■ First-, 2nd- and 3rd-grade teachers in four schools constituting a region of a large school system planned together to develop a regional program of developmental continuity. Their program included the same methods of reporting children's progress and a continuum of experiences and projects suited to the culture and resources in the community.

■ Second-grade teachers wanted to change traditional spelling activities. They informed parents and their principal of why and how they were going to encourage children's writing by experimenting with spelling, discovering patterns, formulating spelling rules and uncovering exceptions to the rules.

With so many diverse directions to go in, a teacher or administrator with previous experience in challenging the system can help to develop clear procedures for beginning the process. Here is one teacher's action plan:

1. State the purpose for change with clarity.
2. Specify the goals and objectives necessary to achieve the purpose.
3. Decide on the scope and breadth of the program.
4. Determine the procedures that must take place to fulfill objectives.
5. Enlist others who are to be involved.
6. Locate resources within the school and the school system.
7. Decide how to evaluate the success of the innovations.

As for Claudia, with Consuela's encouragement, she began to change the curriculum in her classroom. Her first step was to enlist the help of Helen, a kindergarten teacher in the same school. The two decided that they would each try out specific curriculum practices in their classrooms that would cohere with the work in the other. They began by initiating a number of strategies suggested by those advocating a whole language philosophy. They determined what parts of their program and practices they would change and how they would evaluate their success.

Over the next six months, they tried out different ideas, meeting to share their successes and fret over the things they tried that turned out less than wonderfully. They revised plans and made additional changes, supporting one another.

### Communicating

Dewey (1944) believed that unless one could effectively communicate ideas to others, clarity of thought was impossible. Likewise, Claudia and Helen believed that it was important to practice their communicating skills with each other. They took turns describing their program and intentions to each other. As they talked, they described to each other:

■ the purpose, goals and intent of the changes they were going to make
■ some of the possible benefits to children, the school system, parents and teachers
■ the theory and research supporting their program
■ possible costs and cost-benefits that would accrue.

Confident of their ability to articulate their plans clearly, thinking on their feet answering one another's questions, Claudia and Helen began the process of involving others.

### Involving Others

Many teachers have attempted to make changes within their classrooms only to discover great resistance from parents who do not understand what is happening. By involving others, teachers have found other voices that support the changes and can articulate to others the value of these changes for children.

Paul's and Valerie's mothers were regular volunteers in the classroom. Active in the PTA, they had historically worked to support their children's teachers. One day, excited over the stories children had written after their trip to the harbor to watch a ship dock, Claudia explained her excitement to the mothers. "In the past I always had the children fill out workbook pages to gain the concept of subject and verb agreement. This semester Helen and I decided to see if another method, better suited to children's maturation, would work. Because we wanted children to initiate some of their own learning activities, we followed their interest in boats and transportation with a trip to the harbor."

She showed the mothers the skills that the children were accomplishing: "Look at the complexity of sentence structure in these stories. Since the children have prepared these stories for 'publishing,' they have been revised several times. As the children were writing, we discussed some of their initial errors, as things to look for when editing their stories. Among other 'problems' we discussed was the problem of subject and verb agreement. They developed their own lists of hard to spell words, looking up some of the words in the dictionary. If you read all the papers, you will see that there are very few misspelled words and very few grammatical errors. Not only have they demonstrated knowledge of correct usage better than when using worksheets, but they are able to write so much better. These stories demonstrate that the 'whole language' approach that Helen and I are trying has a great deal of potential."

Daily, Claudia and Helen described and explained the changes they were making and why to their parent volunteers. The possibilities of changing the curriculum to be more responsive to young children's development intrigued the parents. Excited by the changes they were observing in the classroom, they in turn talked with other parents.

Claudia started with parents already volunteering in her classroom. The normal ways of contacting parents can be used to communicate. Conferences, home visits, informal contacts via notes, telephone calls or parent bulletin boards are all available to inform parents of a new program. If these traditional modes of communicating are ineffective, ways of changing them can be explored. For example, there have been suggestions that children be involved in parent/teacher conferences. Would that work for some children and their families? Or would a parent volunteer calling on other parents be more effective in communicating than notes forwarded to the home or telephone calls by the teacher?

Both Claudia and Helen found they had a group of parents who brought in resources, worked with individual children and suggested other experiences for the class. This group of parents, with the principal's support, began to contact other parents, helping them to understand that the classroom changes were providing more continuity of experiences for their children.

### Receiving Authorization

Feeling validated by the support and enthusiastic responses of the parents, Claudia and her friend asked to meet with their principal. Buttressed with samples of the children's work, a written statement of their goals and intentions, and reprints of several articles about developmentally appropriate curriculum, they described the changes they had made over the past semester. They asked for authorization to continue developing additional methods of responding to children's developmental needs.

Although many changes can be made in the classroom without authorization, major changes to be instituted will require some type of authorization. Local and state policies, developed in the belief that they will ensure quality and a standard of education for all children under their jurisdiction, would have to be examined and studied. The flexibility of these policies, and the parameters that could not be changed, must be identified. Many changes can be made that fit within the parameters of stated policies, and yet other plans may first require changes in policies.

Different school systems will require authorization from different sources. In Milwaukee, during the beginning days of moving from separate primary grades to a nongraded primary unit, teachers in one school began to eliminate age-grade placement by changing their name plates outside their rooms. They removed the signs saying *Grade 1, 2* and so on to *Ms. Smith, NONGRADED PRIMARY UNIT*. Before they did so, however, they asked their principal for authorization. By getting his approval first, the teachers had a strong supporter when parents and state supervisors asked about the change.

When Ann decided not to report her kindergarten children's progress by checking off competencies achieved, she asked to meet with the school board. Describing and illustrating how she had reported children's progress to parents using narrative systems of anecdotal records, she asked for permission to discard the competency list of separated and isolated skills and continue with her narratives. Ann's strategy of going first to the school board educated this important body about the need for change as well as laid the foundation of necessary support.

Another school district, under authorization from the school board, experimented with a narrative system, but got so bogged down with writing elaborate narratives they requested permission to devise their own developmental lists. As they experimented with the lists, they enlisted parental support and feedback. In the end they developed a form that most teachers, parents and administrators felt really demonstrated children's growth. The teachers in this district discovered that, by seeking permission to experiment and make changes, better communications were established with the school board, as well as with the community.

Convinced by Claudia and Helen's ability to articulate their ideas and by the documentation of children's success and their enthusiasm for learning, the principal agreed to work toward structuring developmental continuity across the school's kindergarten and primary grades. Other teachers were invited to meet with Claudia and Helen and eventually a kindergarten/primary team was formed.

### Expanding

Beginning small seems to guarantee a measure of success. By beginning small, more variables can be controlled. With small beginnings, it is easier to change methods that do not work, refine and polish those that have potential, build the comfort level of all involved, and perfect practices when working with a few teachers or small groups of children. But, if the goal is to provide continuity of children's educational experiences across the preschool and primary grades, then expansion and involvement of many more individuals and groups will be necessary as the ideas take hold.

Expansion of developmental continuity to the upper grades often occurs with successful nongraded primary units or when multi-age groupings are present within a school. Other teachers notice the intense involvement of neighboring children in their own learning, samples of their written work posted in the hallways, as well as children's enhanced achievement. Impressed with the achievement of nearby children, teachers in the upper grades can be involved in continuing to respond to children's developmental needs throughout the elementary school.

As children leave the primary grades, they will continue to respond best to teachers who engage them in active learning, who support their intellectual curiosity and pursuits, and who build on their accomplishments from their primary years. Manning (in press) discusses appropriate curriculum practices in the elementary grades that support children who have been involved in preschool/primary programs of developmental continuity. If developmental continuity is to succeed, then others within the school system and the larger community must be involved and committed to creating a continuous program throughout the preschool/primary and elementary grades that is responsive to children's developmental level.

### Involving Parents

At the very least, parents will need to be informed of changes within a given school. A continuum of communication techniques can inform parents and gain their commitment. These include:

■ *Notes explaining any new process or change in the curriculum.* "Dear Parent," wrote a 1st-grade teacher, knowing parents would be upset with children's invented spelling, "you may note misspelled words in your child's written work. This is because we are asking children to form a habit of writing without worrying about correct form at first. Thus, they are encouraged to write the word as they hear it." She continued to explain the rationale for proceeding in this manner as children are learning to read and write, as well as when and how correct spelling would be a part of their learning about revising, editing and publishing their written work.

■ *An open-door policy for parent observations with continued invitations to visit in the classroom and become involved as volunteers.* One 2nd-grade teacher found that the children in his classroom were not able to do as many projects as he and they wanted because of a lack of parent volunteers. Discussing this dilemma with the children, they decided to go on a campaign to get 100 percent parent involvement.

He and the children started by making a list of all the things a parent could do to assist in supporting the children's classroom activities. They then outlined some of their planned projects and brainstormed some of the ways they thought their parents might help them and other children in the classroom to accomplish their tasks. Some suggestions were the traditional ones of providing materials, helping in the classroom and baking cookies. Others got more original: one child volunteered that his father might be able to videotape their play and another indicated that his father could help them identify the rocks they found in the park.

The teacher then sent a letter home informing parents of the class's campaign and some of the suggestions, asking for their input. As responses were made, a schedule was devised and parents were kept informed of the various projects and types of support that were given through notes, verbal communication and the class newspaper.

■ *Making certain that products are sent home—those that illustrate children's learning, work and progress and clearly communicate the nature of developmentally appropriate curriculum.* A kindergarten teacher attached notes to children's scribbles, describing the progress children made in controlling scribbles and beginning use of symbols to represent reality. She also copied many experience charts, letters or anything else the group dictated. Many of these materials she would duplicate and send home with each child. Books made by the group were also photocopied and forwarded home. In order to foster an understanding of the curriculum, other teachers sent to parents photos of children working together in a group, completed group projects and tape recordings of children singing and reciting poems.

■ *Presentations by teachers at parent meetings to show what the children are learning.*
One kindergarten teacher made a presentation at a PTA meeting describing the class's
unit on panda bears. He had an intriguing display of toy pandas, pictures of the
children visiting the pandas at the zoo, books used in the panda unit and examples of
children's drawings and stories about pandas. His talk explained how the children
got involved in the unit, as well as the concepts about pandas the children had
acquired. The drawings and writings at the beginning of the unit, juxtaposed with
those completed at the end of the unit, demonstrated the children's growth in literacy, as well as in concept development.

When projects involve communication between the preschool and elementary
school, the entire community will need to be involved. Using communications media, speaking to community groups and church organizations can help create a better
understanding of developmental continuity throughout a community. The local press
can be given a description of the program, detailing the rationale and issues involved. Pictures can be shown of children interacting with each other and the materials of the school, and identification can be made of the specific skills children can
gain through these and similar experiences. It is important to document the success
of the program so the public is aware of what is happening.

## Bottom-Up or Top-Down

Obviously, teachers are not the only ones who can make changes. Administrators,
supervisors, principals and state departments of education are as responsible as teachers for providing developmental continuity throughout children's early years.

Principals and child care directors do lead. Gaining the cooperation of two or
three teachers, and beginning to involve parents and the community, they can initiate
developmental continuity throughout an entire school system. Or supervisors can
initiate programs, involving representatives of the child care, preschool community
in developing programs designed to provide children with early educational experiences that continue from the preschool through the primary grades. Regardless, the
need to enlist the commitment of others and to communicate to parents and others in
the community must be met.

With commitment, information about other programs, definitions of developmental
continuity, communication with and involvement of others, and authorization of school
administration, a group of people can commence the process of developing a program
that responds to children's individual needs and allows for continuous growth.

The changes that such a program requires will depend upon how the school
presently functions. Since developmental continuity is more successful with evolutionary change rather than revolutionary change, teachers might start with one idea
and experiment with what changes are required in school organization to achieve
natural flow from preschool through 3rd grade. If children are to be actively involved in their own learning, then space arrangement, daily schedule and the overall
classroom environment will be affected. Although the beginning may be a small one,
eventually how the curriculum is organized and defined will undergo revision. If
children are to be evaluated on how well they are developing according to their own
pace and style of learning, then new ways of assessing and reporting this growth
must be developed. Rapid changes in all these areas are not likely to take place;
small steps in one part will effect changes in another area.

# CHAPTER 3

# *Continuity of Organization*

❝ Helen and I are beginning to see some important changes in children's work and progress," Claudia reports excitedly to Consuela later that year. "Even better, Valerie's and Paul's parents are helping us explain to other parents what is evolving. The principal is in our classrooms almost daily, encouraging us to try new ideas, and he is telling other teachers about what is happening. The principal is even beginning to suggest some structural and organizational changes he thinks might facilitate our successes. You know, Consuela, it's a lot of work."

"Yes," replies Consuela, "but isn't it up to us to find the most exciting ways for each child to succeed? You are lucky to have found an interested colleague, such a supportive principal and eager parents so early. I had to change schools before I could make these ideas succeed. Your principal seems to be aware that more steps will need to be taken and is willing to be a part of the change process. ❞

To make changes, teachers do need the support of a system that is willing to make alterations in the structure and organization of the school. There are many ways to make such changes, but important components of the change process are: 1) creating a school-based management team with all parties represented that advises, assists and supports the classroom teachers' efforts; 2) restructuring the organization of the kindergarten/primary unit; 3) developing strong links with preschools in order to provide smooth transitions for children entering this school for the first time; 4) establishing continuous support and communication among teachers, administrators, parents, community agencies and businesses.

## SCHOOL MANAGEMENT TEAM

Creating a school management team of teachers, parents and other school personnel is often a first step. During initial phases of structuring developmental continuity, the team may start with only a couple of teachers, a principal and parents. As the program grows, the team needs to grow with it. During the program's evaluation, new interests and needs will arise, needs that can be met by representatives from parent groups, other teachers, administrators, members of child care and preschool community, and/or community agencies and businesses.

In one school Jim and Felicity, a kindergarten and 1st-grade teacher, had begun to work together to plan units so that their curriculum would make more sense to the children in their classes. Before too long, two of the parents became interested and began working with them to get parent involvement for their projects. Seeing the enthusiasm, other teachers began to "borrow" their ideas and soon the principal began to change teachers' meetings, so that more total school planning was taking place.

As changes in curriculum were occurring, children's interest in exploring topics took them beyond the classroom into the community. The teachers had always "taken trips" into the community, but some children wanted to explore more about how certain businesses were run. One of the parents on the team suggested that perhaps her boss could help. Indeed he did, and he even got some support from his business associates in the chamber of commerce. Although at first "the team" was made up of Jim and Felicity because of mutual planning, more and more people became interested. At this point, the principal decided to form a school management team, just to coordinate the many activities. Today, teachers in that school often form a small subgroup with parents for planning, but they find the support of the management helpful in many ways.

A management team serves a number of functions. The purpose and tasks of this team will evolve, but the original tasks will be to:

- facilitate and coordinate the cooperation of classroom staffs within the kindergarten/primary unit
- establish methods of communicating with the child care and preschool community
- enlist and coordinate the services of other appropriate groups as children's needs demand
- assess the success of the process
- read about and visit other programs and research projects that are organized for developmental continuity.

The school management team, while fostering communication between and among those involved in creating developmental continuity, also serves as a source of support and encouragement for teachers' and parents' efforts to build curriculum that continuously responds to children's development. When teachers' decisions about classroom procedures are in conflict with others and/or with children's apparent needs, the school management team would serve as the forum for final decisions. Finally, the team is responsible for coordinating the teachers' goals with those of the child care/preschool community, the local system and state policies.

State and local school boards set policies to ensure quality education for the children under their jurisdiction. The team's responsibilities would include study of these policies and recommendations for change when there are apparent needs. Guidelines for restructuring should first be made within stated policies.

For example, if the local school authorities require that evaluations of children be made using uniform report cards, then the reporting process, at first, will have to fall within these guidelines. Evaluation procedures using a more developmentally appropriate reporting system, however, should be begun and shared with parents, other teachers and administrators. After generating this support, the school management team can approach the local school board with a proposal either to allow for an exception to the existing grading or to examine its current policy with the view of revising the policy.

The restructuring of schools must be done in a way that allows continuous opportunities for renewal. As changes are made, part of the team's responsibility would be to assess the communication process both within and across units and the larger community. Periodically, the team would determine if the various groups responsible for children's development have adequate representation on the team.

Another important role of the school management team has to do with professional development. Additional training and education for teachers, administrators, paraprofessionals, parents and staff of community agencies serving this school community would be examined. Workshops, university course work, lectures, television productions, books and articles would be made available, and topics for discussion sessions identified and planned.

The management team would also develop cooperative arrangements with university personnel with the prospect of conducting joint research projects, providing mutually beneficial opportunities for preservice teachers and extending opportunities for children. If a university professor becomes a member of the management team, both institutions benefit. The school can profit from the expertise of university personnel and can, in return, offer the university research opportunities and better experiences for preservice teachers. School-university partnerships also enable university professors to keep in contact with the day-to-day workings of the school and issues confronting classroom teachers.

## RESTRUCTURING THE KINDERGARTEN/PRIMARY UNIT

If each child is to have an initial school experience that allows for a smooth transition from his/her earlier experiences, then some of the traditional ways schools have been organized will need to be changed. Different methods of grouping, scheduling, promotion, staffing and reporting will be necessary to break the rigid barriers of age/grade grouping.

### Grouping
A curriculum that responds to children's continuing development depends on a community of learners who progress at their own individual pace across the preschool and primary units. The unit consists of the children and teachers in the preschool and primary grades for whom the management team is responsible. The unit will cut across age ranges, but may vary from school to school. Size of the unit, grouping within the unit and teacher/group arrangement are important considerations.

■ *Size of the Unit*. The unit must be small enough so that teaching/learning can be personalized. Although size might vary from school to school, 100 children per unit is a workable figure. A smaller unit allows parents, teachers and other school personnel to know all members of the unit and to work together as a community.

■ *Grouping Within the Unit*. Multi-age grouping is based on the idea that children learn from one another. "In families, villages, settlements, neighborhoods, and even transient settings such as during travel, children imitate, instruct, direct, follow, interrogate, and respond to one another's knowledge, ideas and feelings" (Katz, Evangelou & Hartman, 1990, p. vii).

The British call multi-age classes "family groupings," meaning that just as in a family, there are children of different ages, with different expectations for each child. Children are usually grouped in ages of 4-5-6, 5-6-7 or 6-7-8. Grouping is flexible and, as older children are ready to move into a new group, younger children come into the group. With a small number of new children each year to acclimate to the classroom, teachers and children begin each year with less trauma and adjustment.

Organizing classrooms with multi-age groups of children provides greater opportunities for meeting the individual needs of children. Children in these groups are believed to benefit from being with both older and younger peers. Younger children benefit from the support of older ones, and older children benefit from helping and teaching younger ones. A 5-year-old, for example, can get help from an older child in figuring out a story sequence while the older child practices skills of explaining and clarifying.

With all this flexibility, there is no need for retention in grade or special promotion to the next grade. Each child's developmental needs can be met by the greater flexibility inherent in multi-age groupings.

■ *Same Teacher/Same Group.* Allowing the same teacher to stay with a kindergarten class throughout the kindergarten and primary grades is another way of structuring flexibility. In this way, relationships between and among children and their teacher are strengthened. Everyone knows one another and trusts one another. The time usually spent at the beginning of the year in becoming acquainted is invested more profitably in building on summer experiences.

Keeping teacher and children together for several years allows teachers to build on children's previous experiences and gives children time to grow. Because many children spurt ahead in some skills but lag behind in others, being with the same group over time permits both teacher and children time to meet individual needs. A teacher explained it this way: "At the end of 1st grade Robert still wasn't reading, and he wasn't much interested in learning either. On the other hand, his progress in math skills was amazing. But that seemed to happen almost overnight. Robert and I know and trust each other, so we know that we will find the way to help him master reading, which may also seem to happen suddenly."

Transitions from one grade to the next are smoother, for no time is wasted in getting to know one another. The teacher knows each child and everyone knows each other. After summer vacation, coming back to school takes on the spirit of a reunion, and resumption of school tasks begins again naturally.

Teachers are also able to do more with their group. A 2nd-grade teacher in Boston, who had stayed with the same group since kindergarten, took the class on a skiing trip to Vermont. She admitted that usually 2nd-graders would not be ready for an overnight trip away from home and parents, but they were a family. She knew each child very well and each child knew and trusted her.

Although having a teacher stay with the same group of children over two or three years has very positive aspects, it is wise to be alert to situations where such a model may not work for a group of children or for a single child. Parents may also object to having their child with the same teacher, fearing the child may be "stuck" in an unfavorable situation. Before adopting such a plan, the management team would need to have alternative plans for adjusting the arrangement if it is not working and communicate such a plan to the parents. When flexibility is the rule and the goal is for children to be in developmentally appropriate classrooms, then a primary unit may find that certain groups of children function better with a different teacher each year and with changing classmates. A single child might have a better experience the second year with a different teacher because of personality differences.

■ *Flexible Grouping.* Flexible grouping within each classroom takes place. One 3rd-grade classroom had no permanent groupings; groups were formed for specific purposes and projects. When the goals were achieved or the project completed, groups were reorganized. Children belonged to more than one group in any given time period.

For example, during one month Jennifer joined two friends every Monday morning to discuss their "reading for fun" weekend books. During project time, she and three others experimented with making quicksand in a geographic land area they had simulated. The project took three days to complete. She was assigned to a third group of four students responsible for illustrating their findings, as the entire class examined the moon phases for the month. She and five other students worked together on distinguishing between words beginning with "wh" and "w." By the end of the week, all six students successfully mastered the skill. Several times during the day/week, she participated with the entire class for instruction, discussion or paper-and-pencil work projects.

With this flexible grouping philosophy, the teacher was able to accommodate diverse interests, learning rates and styles. Almost always, there was some assignment to support children's desire to work with special friends. As children expressed interest in special projects or events from their academic studies, they learned to examine problems with students who shared their enthusiasm. At times, children were permitted to work independently on a project of special interest, becoming the class "expert" on that topic. The teacher also carefully assigned groups where children worked cooperatively to achieve specific goals. Sometimes the groups were a deliberate mix; other times children were grouped by ability or skill level, depending upon the learning (Barbour, 1990).

### Scheduling

Providing developmental continuity for all children may require changes in traditional scheduling. If children are to acquire knowledge by exploring, manipulating and experimenting, large blocks of time must be designated for activities. Within those large blocks of time, a variety of activities and choices may be available. Activities would include both indoor and outdoor events.

For example, Steve's 2nd-grade class schedule usually proceeded in the following manner. The morning schedule began with general group time to discuss the day's plans, establish necessary routines, and provide important instructions or information to assist the children as they began their group or individual projects. Reading/writing workshop was followed by math/science workshop. During these blocks of time, children would select activities or projects to begin, work on or complete. The activity or project themes were related to science, social studies, literature and/or mathematics content.

At times, a theme might be related in one workshop area almost exclusively, as when the children were studying different types of fairy tales. For a week during reading/writing workshop time, they investigated similarities and differences in fairy tale formats. At the same time, science/math workshop time was spent on investigating the concept of volume, or "how much different containers can hold." During another week, the entire morning was given to one workshop as children were involved in a unit on insects. Groups of children read about, wrote about and did some experiments about insects of their choice.

During workshop time, Steve helped individuals or small groups with reading books, writing their original stories, setting up mathematical or science problems, or developing a particular skill. As children worked together, they had time to read by themselves, to each other or to the teacher; to write; to gather information related to the theme and/or to work on particular skills. At the end of the morning, Steve always called the group together for summary of the morning's events, listening to stories and poems, or group singing.

The afternoon schedule consisted of social studies and personal project time. Special topics of particular interest to children were selected, with some time for children to work on a "creative" project of their choice or to continue a project started in the morning. One "inventor" made a special doorbell. Another created games for his friends to play. Woodworking, sewing and craft projects were but a few of the products created at this time. Some children read for leisure, others wrote. At one point, a group wrote a play and followed through on its production. Art, music, drama, dance and physical education were pursued within the class as well as taught by specialists outside the classroom. For some of these activities, children met with other children from different classes who had similar interests or special talents. Afternoon dismissal activities included a summary of the day's events, consideration of home projects to extend and reinforce learning and skills, and/or instructions on locating materials for the next day's events.

Such a scheduling plan could also permit kindergarten children to move more gradually into a full day. Napping arrangements could be made for those children who still needed more quiet or rest time in the afternoon. For children whose parents were at home, arrangements could be made for them to move gradually from a half-day kindergarten to a full-day kindergarten.

In this scheduling plan, 6-, 7- and 8-year-olds could gradually move toward participating in projects and creative activities outside the classroom with other children from the unit who have similar interests or with a similar age group. The oldest and more developed children could also have some experiences with children in the older age units. If developmental continuity is important, then such scheduling plans would allow younger children to have the security of only one or two teachers and only one classroom space to contend with, but allow older children to gradually experience learning from different instructors and with different peer groups. Thus, children would move into an organizational pattern appropriate for the next stage of development in a continuous and fluid manner.

Some schools have been experimenting with various ways to group children for better instruction. T. Marjorie Oberlander (1989) describes her experiences with mixing 5-, 6- and 7-year-olds in one class, with the same teacher following the 5-year-olds until they moved into the next unit. The schedule allows for half-day kindergartners, with one group joining the class in the morning and another group joining them in the afternoon. The curriculum provides concrete hands-on experiences for children, with a whole language approach as the means for teaching reading and writing. Science and social studies are integrated into special units that are rotated to avoid duplication. Multi-age grouping allows for cooperative learning, peer tutoring, integrated curriculum and a chance for teachers to assure developmentally appropriate activities (Oberlander, 1989).

## Promotion
With continuous entry into the kindergarten/primary unit, there would be continuous exit from that unit as well; that is, when children reached age 8 or whatever top age the unit is structured for, they would be promoted or would move into the next unit. If the middle school unit is also designed for the success of all children, then those children who were not ready to spend the entire day in the middle school structure would initially spend part of the day in the primary unit—much like kindergarten children who initially spend only half days in the school environment.

Although children learn and develop in different ways and at varying rates, there are some bench marks for the next stage/age. If movement is fluid and continuous, then promotion into the next stage should be natural, with no expectation that all children will have the same knowledge, skill development or social/emotional development. There are expectations, however, that all children will have learned fundamental reading, computational and problem-solving skills. They will also have learned fundamental skills for working/interacting with others, operating with independence and responding in an emotionally appropriate manner.

Retention and transitional classrooms, with the negative aspects that too often result in unfortunate labeling and early tracking of children, would be eliminated. Children who were not able to move full time into the next unit, however, might spend part of their day in the primary unit, working on appropriate intellectual, social or physical tasks that assist them in making a smooth transition into the middle school unit.

### Class Size

The National Association of Elementary School Principals (1990), in accordance with recent research on class size, has recommended the following child/adult ratio and maximum class size:

- For 3-, 4-, 5-year-olds: 2 adults to 20 children, ratio with a class size of 20
- For 6-, 7-, 8-year-olds: 1 adult to 15 children, ratio with a class size of 20
- For at-risk children: 1 adult to 15 children, ratio with a class size of 15. (NAESP, 1990, pp. 9-10)

Simply reducing class size will not make a difference, unless:

- the strategies used in the classroom do provide for individualization
- the children are able to learn through hands-on experiences
- there are opportunities for social interaction with other children, other adults and materials.

With freedom of activity and belief that children should initiate and direct their own learning, it is evident that larger class sizes could only negate flexibility of scheduling, multi-age groupings, flexibility of grouping and, most important, ample opportunities for productive child/child and adult/child interactions.

### Staffing of the Classroom

In each of the classrooms across the kindergarten/primary units, there should be a teacher and a paraprofessional who are primarily responsible for the child's educational experiences. If the educational needs of all children are to be met, however, the child's physical welfare, social/emotional development and moral development will need to be supported.

With flexible scheduling and grouping patterns, children may at times be engaged in activities under the supervision of other teachers, parents, specialists, administrators, social workers or community personnel. In a school where the developmental needs of children are met in a continuous manner, this additional support should not be segmented but rather be part of the total classroom program. For example, children who need a quiet space and a single adult for specific purposes would be able to receive support according to the child's requirements, rather than at the convenience of adult time schedules. Children who are able to function within the classroom would not be pulled out from productive classroom activities, but would receive additional support within the classroom context.

## Reporting Progress

A different procedure is needed to report the progress of children. The current practice of reporting children's learning by comparing standardized test scores of one group with those of another group is contrary to the notion of different growth patterns and rates. Children, parents and society at large have a right to know "how the schools are doing," but reporting standardized test scores does little to inform parents or the community of each child's progress.

More informative reports of children's progress are based on observations, interviews and collections of children's work. If children are involved in mapping their own progress, they, like their parents, will be aware of their increasing knowledge and skills. Charting children's growth and accomplishments through observations and interviews illustrates progression to the next stage of development and achievement more accurately than standardized test scores. If progression is not evident, then these methods also give a better indication as to what steps might be taken to assure positive growth.

Goodlad (1984) suggests that reorganizing schools would give teachers and children a greater opportunity for a . . .

continuous assessment of each child's progress as a thinking, social, reasonably self-assured person. The vertical organization of each unit of 100 children or less who stay together with approximately the same team of teachers over a period of four years facilitates a developmental view of the child and provides the necessary time for assessment, diagnosis, and relatively long-term interventions. The availability of a highly trained head teacher in each unit adds to the likelihood of sound diagnoses and subsequent programmatic adjustments. Much can be done to redesign the program of a 6-year-old appearing to be having difficulties so that progress in all areas is proceeding nicely by the age of 8. The present choppy, graded organization of schools is not conducive to the identification and redirection of developmental deficiencies and irregularities. (pp. 333-334)

## Organizing Materials, Supplies and People

A way for school systems to organize materials, supplies and people is necessary. A central materials room within a school unit, as well as space within each classroom, is helpful. Expensive materials, not needed in each classroom every day, would be rotated among classes when interests or needs arise. A transportation unit might require extra large or unit blocks and specific materials for road construction. Special materials might be required because a harbor is being built in the sand table. Teachers would not use these materials every day but would reserve them for when the unit is being studied.

Most schools have media centers with special thematic material, as well as libraries of good children's literature. Teachers also use the public libraries to enhance their book and material selections around certain themes. A central materials room in each unit would have available some extra books and stories in basal readers marked for difficulty level, unit themes and interest, as well as reference lists and materials lists.

Resource people, as well, need to be available for teachers. A system moving toward developmental continuity would have teachers meet with all music, art, physical education and other special needs resource teachers and personnel to coordinate the programmatic needs and changes in the kindergarten/primary unit. The management team would assist teachers, principal and parents to determine how best to work together with resource persons to facilitate developmental continuity for children.

## STRONG LINKS WITH PRESCHOOLS

Even if children are from the same community, they are likely to have had very different experiences before entering school. If children are to make transitions to their new school in a comfortable way, then teachers and caregivers need to understand the prior experiences of the children they will teach. This makes communication between the management team and the area preschool and child care communities essential.

The management team at the school would take responsibility for establishing links between the preschool and primary grades. Child care workers, teachers, parents and administrators can cooperate in a number of ways to structure smooth transitions for children from their preschool or child care experience to the kindergarten and primary grades. These involve:

- communicating with parents and other teachers
- preparing children for the transition
- developing compatible administrative practices.

### Communicating with Parents and Other Teachers

Many parents are actively involved in their children's preschool and child care experiences. They often see and talk with their child's teachers on a daily basis, as well as volunteer in the classroom and serve on advisory and policy boards. Parents need to be encouraged to continue being involved as their children move into the elementary school.

Providing linkages with the child care or preschool teachers where parents have placed their children requires different approaches to establishing communication. As kindergarten and primary school teachers begin the process, it does not mean all schools will be involved initially. A parent, a child care worker and a teacher can begin the communication process with the intent of providing smoother transitions from one setting to another. As good communication patterns and smoother transitions are provided for a few of the children, other people can be involved. As adults become more adept at making "schools fit the child" rather than making the "child fit the school," different models and approaches to the process will emerge.

The communication process can begin with visits, organizing meetings, sharing newsletters, serving on boards and sharing records.

- *Home Visits.* Making home visits is one way teachers get to know parents better. Although the potential of such visits is yet to be fully realized, home visits provide extensive information about children and how they function in a family setting (Powell, 1990).

It is also true that when teachers and child care workers arrange visits to each other's workplace, they have greater understanding of the children's experiences in both settings. From such visits, each would begin to understand the child's environment and how the structure of each day progresses. Observing children function in a different environment is an added benefit. Teachers can observe how a child who will be entering their class relates with other children and adults. Child care workers can observe how their children are adapting to the new situation, as well as how other children seem to adapt. Questions would be asked as to what seems to be working well for the children and what might be done differently when a child is having a difficult time.

■ *Organized Meetings.* Meetings should be arranged for child care workers and teachers to discuss their ideas, philosophies and goals for providing the best opportunities they can for children with whom they work. The meetings are more productive when they have a purpose and goal. Various meeting formats can be used, depending on those involved and the needs for establishing good working relationships. Informal meetings provide opportunities for open discussion about specific issues; more formal meetings may include a speaker who discusses some current topic of mutual concern. It might be appropriate for teachers and child care workers to attend workshops and/or take courses together to increase their understanding about child development and appropriate practices. At the very least, knowledge of available workshops and courses should be shared with all.

■ *Sharing Newsletters.* Schools and child care centers often send newsletters home to parents as a means of maintaining contact and communication. These letters can be exchanged between the elementary school and child care and preschool programs. By exchanging newsletters, the personnel in each setting will be aware of the information and the special events each provides to parents. Articles, reviews or summaries of books, and notices of upcoming events pertaining to children's needs are often included in these newsletters to parents. Knowledge about the experiences provided for children in various settings can assist others in extending these experiences or in preparing children for events to come.

■ *Board Members.* The composition of the board can be an important factor in building developmental continuity. Kindergarten teachers should be invited to sit on preschool or child care advisory boards, while preschool teachers can be involved in the policy advisory boards or management teams of the elementary school. Other advisory board members will then be up-to-date on what is happening in classrooms and teachers will play a role in board decisions.

■ *Joint Records.* In order to provide appropriate curricula for children, teachers need to exchange pertinent information about children's growth. Preschool staff and the school management team might cooperate in record transfer from the preschool to the kindergarten or in the development of joint records that follow children across the preschool and primary grades. Preschool teachers could also write letters to the receiving schools in the spring, listing the names of incoming children and communicating information about their preschool program (State of Connecticut, 1988).

### Preparing Children
With openness of communication between the elementary school and feeder preschools and child care centers, teachers from both settings can design ways of preparing children for their transition into the kindergarten.

One kindergarten class made a booklet describing what they had learned in kindergarten for each child in the feeder preschool. In this booklet, the children dictated and illustrated the things they had done in kindergarten and described what they had learned.

In another school, the management team made a video of their school. They started with the ride to school, and followed a child throughout the school day. As a part of the tape, they interviewed kindergarten children who described what they liked best about kindergarten and how kindergarten was different from preschool. Copies of the video were sent to the four feeder preschools.

Preschool teachers have found that children's enactment of going to kindergarten is helpful in smoothing the transition. Children take turns pretending to ride the bus, to sit and listen to a story, and to eat lunch in a cafeteria.

Puppets were created by one preschool teacher to represent the kindergarten teacher, principal, cafeteria worker and kindergarten children. Using the puppet stage the group had often used in the past, she encouraged the children to play "going to kindergarten." She used one of the puppets to correct misconceptions, give feedback and keep the play moving.

Concerned that her children wouldn't know how to adapt to some of the routines of the big school, a teacher took a few children at a time to visit. The kindergarten children served as guides to the visitors as they toured the whole school; met the principal, the cafeteria workers and others; and visited in the classroom. The kindergartners sat with their guests for snack time and played with them at recess. Upon return, the preschoolers discussed their feelings and role-played situations that were of concern.

In another area, people from the school made field trips to the preschools. The librarian, cook, custodian and representatives from the kindergarten and primary grades visited the preschools in the area. They introduced themselves and their school to the children. Some schools have even arranged for children to ride the school bus with their parents from the preschool to the elementary school.

Children who have never been to preschool or child care should be identified by the management team so that both parents and children can be invited to share some of the same experiences.

## SUPPORT AND COMMUNICATION LINKS TO THE COMMUNITY

Society today differs drastically from society of the 1900s when the present school organizations were formed. The family may still be the mainstay for any youngster; however, the family unit today differs from the nuclear and extended family units prevalent during the early 1900s. The traditional models of parent/school relationships may not be sufficient to meet the demands for educating today's children to become socially responsible, mentally and physically competent, and motivated to become productive citizens.

Large school systems have been organized in ways that take a sense of ownership and responsibility away from parents and local community people. Even though community agencies offer a variety of support systems for parents and children, this support is often fragmented and children are not served as well as they might be through a more cohesive system.

Businesses are beginning to become aware that they have a real stake in the education of tomorrow's citizens. A prosperous economy depends upon a larger, better educated and adaptable workforce. Yet the services or benefits that could accrue from a business' involvement in schools may remain unfulfilled for two reasons: 1) results are not immediate and readily assessed in quantitative ways and 2) the school's goals and business' goals are not compatible (MacDowell, 1989).

Shirley Brice Heath's (1983) ethnographic study on communities and classrooms points out how different cultures support different models for children's behavior that may or may not support school behaviors. Thus, children from homes whose cultural expectations differ from school expectations may be hampered from achieving the intellectual competence of which they are capable. Today's children from a wide range of family structures bring quite different "cultural capital" into classrooms where the skills and expectations for being successful in school have not changed that much since the turn of the century.

Some children have been exposed to more extensive family and community experiences than others. These experiences require them to adapt their language patterns to different social situations. These children already know that there are acceptable ways to talk to parents that are to be altered when talking to someone else. They have had many opportunities listening to siblings, parents and significant adults adapt language to different situations. For example, their mother uses a rather simple language pattern to speak to the baby, but when talking to the father uses more complex sentences; when explaining a situation to the minister, she uses a more formal speech. These children have been listened to and expected to respond in increasingly more complex ways.

In all homes, children observe written language; however, the emphasis on using written language as a means of communicating varies widely. Many "at-risk" students are from cultural groups that place more emphasis on oral language and use written language in more restricted ways. The school culture even early on focuses on written language. Thus, children whose home culture focuses on written language are at an advantage.

Children from all backgrounds who are academically successful have participated in activities beyond school and home that demand a complexity of oral and written skills. They may have participated in preschool story hours at the library. They may have belonged to various community organizations, such as scouting; participated in athletics; taken specialized lessons, such as art, music, drama; even participated in work-related activities (Heath & McLaughlin, 1989). Successful participation in these beyond-school experiences provide them with skills to become more language proficient, more self-assured, more physically and socially competent. These competencies usually support them as they approach the academic demands of formal schooling. Since such services already exist for some children, Heath and McLaughlin (1989) suggest that schools move beyond "the role of 'deliverer' of educational services to the role of 'broker of the multiple services'" to all children (p. 579).

### Family Support

Schools traditionally have considered establishing good home/school relationships as part of their responsibility. With changing societal demands on parents, however, this task becomes more difficult. When school personnel give the impression that children are failing because "something is wrong with the child or the parent," then adversarial roles develop. Viewing their role as "brokers," management teams would try to break down these barriers and build bridges, so that eventually all parents see the importance of involvement in their children's growth and development, as well as the contributions they have to make toward their children's education. Just as children have different levels of needs, parents are also at different levels of ability to respond to their children's needs.

Many successful programs for parental involvement exist (Brandt, 1989; Galen, 1991; Vandergrift & Greene, 1992). Part of the management team's task would be to keep informed about these programs, and to model efforts for increasing parental involvement based on how others have been successful. The team would be able to articulate the goals of developmental continuity: that all children will achieve academic, social and physical skills, though the rate of progress may not be the same for all children, nor will progress always be in even patterns. There should be goal-setting for parental involvement, the ultimate goal being to convince *all* parents that success for their children requires their active support and cooperation, even if the outward manifestation of that support is different. Then the task of the team would be to determine what beginning steps need to be taken and how to assess the progress being made toward achieving the ultimate goal.

## Community Support

Community support might begin with one classroom, one or two teachers, a few parents and a supportive administrator. As the team approaches the task of being a "broker," the success of developmental continuity will ultimately depend upon children receiving the benefits of community cooperation in providing appropriate expertise and services. At some point, the management team will need to expand to include a "community resource" person who can determine how, when and where health, library, tutoring, counseling, athletic, artistic, social and other appropriate services can be provided to all children in the school.

Various innovative community support programs are in operation today. At times the project is all encompassing, as in the Yale Child Welfare Research Program (Rapoport, 1985). Nevertheless, many schools are asking for the assistance of diverse community agencies. For example, universities are supporting college students as they tutor, act as mentors and sponsor children's clubs in a particular school or group of schools. Often a university offers special seminars to the student-tutors where they can examine the impact of the services they render.

Enthusiasm and commitment can start the process of community support. As the team expands, however, members will need to determine what is achievable as well as profitable for the success of the children in school.

## Business Support

Businesses have successfully contributed to the schools in their community in various ways. Some have contributed equipment, such as computers, or money for specific changes in curriculum or in major school reform. Some have cooperated in developing kindergarten programs (Severn, 1992). In other instances, businesses have provided incentive programs for students to get better grades or to achieve on certain tasks, such as reading a number of books and sharing them with parents and teachers. Not all ventures have been successful, especially those planned by administrators and business leaders without regard to those who must implement the project or who will be recipients of their efforts.

For a school concerned with implementing programs in a fashion consistent with developmentally appropriate practices, these business partnerships must be developed out of the needs of the particular students in the schools. The school management team would assess not only the students' needs but also the business' potential for providing that need.

It is best to inaugurate business support for schools by becoming acquainted with the institutions involved. Team members should visit the place of business in the spirit of "what can we do for each other." Business people would visit the schools, or even volunteer, to become better acquainted with the goals of the school, the staff and students, and current methods of education. They would thus gain better insights into the schooling process. This reciprocity would equip those involved with better knowledge of the resources, ideas and commitments that each party could bring to the partnership. Roles and resources might change from year to year, depending on the needs of students and the commitment of the businesses. MacDowell (1989) gives some general guidelines for establishing positive school/business partnerships:

1. Select those areas of the curriculum or unit that appeal to the business or where there is some expertise within the company.
2. Make sure the goals of the school and the company are compatible.
3. Familiarize the company with the realities of schooling.
4. Provide for measuring the success of the involvement within the appropriate goals for student growth.
5. Consider a diverse type of involvement for the company, besides contributions of money and materials. (p. 9)

With successful partnerships, the school management teams should eventually have a representative from the business community, in order to keep influential leaders aware of the importance of providing quality education for all children.

If developmental continuity is to be provided for tomorrow's children, then schools will have to make changes. It is not possible for a single teacher to bring about the kinds of changes that are required. A teacher concerned and committed to improving education for all children, however, can seek out other like-minded teachers, parents and administrators and begin to experiment with changes in the school's organization. A small management team can restructure a single kindergarten/primary unit, organize links with preschools and child care centers whose children will be a part of the unit, establish strong communication with those involved initially—teachers, administrators and parents—and later establish ties with community agencies and businesses. When change results in children having greater success and more positive attitudes toward school, then more people can be involved and encouraged to participate.

# CHAPTER 4

# *Continuity of Curriculum*

**"** Helen and I are struggling, but we're beginning to see why you get so excited about your developmental curriculum," says Claudia.

"It's always exciting to see change in the classroom," replies Consuela. "Children get so involved in their projects, they ask very stimulating questions, and I find that I'm constantly learning new things myself. Make no mistake, you'll find it's hard work! I'm always planning, thinking about what new challenges to offer, learning about each child and his/her growth. Worrying when Jenny isn't grasping that containers hold the same amount in spite of their shape, when the rest of the class has long ago comprehended. But then, I'm dazzled when suddenly she exclaims, 'Wow, every one of these containers holds three of whatever I put in. They must *really* be the same size.' That's much more invigorating than following some predetermined curriculum guide with its predetermined scope and sequence charts."

"But I still worry," Claudia asserts. "Those scope and sequence charts are necessary if children are going to learn the skills they need. After all, school is a place for children to learn, and today there is a great deal of pressure for them to learn more if we expect them to succeed. All the excitement we feel about learning new things may not be enough in today's marketplace."

"Believe me, you'll begin to see children are learning the skills on those charts and lots more besides. Let me tell you about last week," answers Consuela. "We've been focusing on developing our observation skills, so the children have been bringing in things, looking at them, comparing how they looked to the naked eye and how they looked under the microscope. Monday, several of them brought in leaves because they found them so colorful. I may not see anything new in fall leaves, but the children haven't seen as many falls as I have, and they love collecting them. When you think about it, fall is still new to them. New, yet familiar at the same time. Maybe it's the familiarity of working with leaves that enables children to feel secure enough to risk learning something new like graphing.

"At first they began to make comparisons like they had been doing and we listed all sorts of characteristics they observed: colors, pointed or round ends, numbers of points a leaf had, short or long leaves. We identified those the children knew the names of, and children volunteered to go to the library and find books about trees. Other children volunteered to try to find some different leaves to bring into the classroom.

"That afternoon the children began to categorize the leaves according to the characteristics, and during math, since we had begun a graphing unit, children formed groups to make graphs of the different characteristics, labeling them from large to small, pointed to round, light to dark.

"As the project unfolded, children began to identify their leaves with trees, using the books we had found in the library. A walk around the school yard helped us to identify which trees grew near the school and to compare the pictured tree to the real tree. Children continued to bring leaves from home or a walk in the woods with their parents.

"During group times, children shared what they were discovering and posed questions of what else they could find out. I read the poem *Trees* by Kilmer and the book *The Apple Tree* by Parnall. During writing time, we first composed a poem together about leaves and then children wrote their own poems or stories. Some children illustrated their work; others chose to paint a picture to express what they learned about trees. I'm collecting their work into a book that they will be able to borrow and take home to share with their parents. The children have already started to summarize and share what each one has learned from his study of leaves. This summary helps me keep track of the individual children's learning.

"As children are discovering new trees, the focus has begun to center on what kinds of trees exist and where. I'm thinking of expanding this unit since environmental concerns is an important topic and the importance of trees to our lives and to our environment will fit nicely into the curriculum requirements.

"Just sharing this experience with you makes me realize how much more my children learned last week, than if I had used only the basal series or the science textbooks. They counted and measured leaves, made and gained meaning from a bar graph. Each selected at least one book to read, which they shared in small groups. In reading we are focusing on how authors indicate setting. Among other things, the children noted where the trees were found and how the authors showed that in their books. In writing their poems and stories, many were able to use different and creative descriptors. I tend not to put great stress on grammar, but occasionally I will share what great adjectives we've used and how such words help to make pictures more clearly in the minds of our readers.

"They also gained a lot of experience working together in groups. The power of this informal give-and-take communication is invaluable. While working on group projects, children find it necessary to make their ideas clear to others. Of course, this doesn't always happen naturally. We do spend time discussing how to clarify our ideas for others.

"You know, taking time to actually document in writing what the children have done has uncovered something else they learned. To find the names of the trees and other information they wanted, I realize that the librarian, or in some cases the parents, showed them how to use a table of contents and an index. I'm going to follow up on that skill and add it to my next lesson plan. I need to know which ones are skilled in this area and which ones will need more guidance from me.

"A developmental curriculum considers the expectations of the school very seriously, perhaps even more seriously, but these expectations are not translated into lists of isolated skills or scope and sequence charts children need to master. Isolation may be the real difference. A developmental curriculum does not isolate anything—not expectations of the schools, not skills, not content, not children. The expectations of the school, as mastery of skills, are important, but only as part of the whole idea, not in isolation from meaningful content. And certainly not isolated from what children find meaningful, or from their needs and abilities. I begin with the children—knowledge of them helps me decide what skills I'll introduce, which ones I'll ask the children to practice, and how and when. **"**

46

## CREATING MEANINGFUL CURRICULUM

In order to create meaningful curriculum for children, teachers need to understand societal expectations of the function of schooling, as well as what is appropriate instruction for children. Each school and each school system have stated goals and objectives for children's achievement usually developed by state departments of education, school boards, groups of teachers within a system, or parent groups. These expectations must be developmentally appropriate if they are to ensure quality educational experiences for all children. A school's or a system's expectations, when stated as appropriate goals and objectives for children's learning or through scope and sequence charts, are necessary in providing standards of excellence.

Developmentally appropriate expectations of a school system or individual school within a system offer teachers a solid framework for curriculum planning. Rather than limiting teacher or child choice, such a framework ensures that all children will have equal access to quality educational experiences. By following and adhering to appropriate expectations of the school and striving to change inappropriate ones, teachers know that their curriculum will: 1) reflect the values of the community, 2) provide all children with the same curriculum opportunities and 3) offer a balance of goals and objectives from each subject area discipline.

**66** Honestly," says Consuela, "I do follow the expectations of the school as I plan my curriculum. It is just that if I followed these expectations exactly as stated they would have little meaning to the children I teach. Each teacher needs to figure out how to make the expectations of the school meaningful to each individual group of children and each child within the group. **99**

Meaningfulness is all important. There doesn't seem to be any doubt about the need for teachers to make the things they teach meaningful to children. "Research indicated, that the more meaningful, the more deeply or elaboratively processed, the more situated in context and personal knowledge an event is, the more readily it is understood, learned, and remembered" (Iran-Nejad, McKeachie & Berliner, 1990, p. 511).

Curriculum that continuously responds to the children and holds meaning for them may, as Consuela suggested, begin with the children themselves. It probably is more accurate, however, to say that a curriculum with developmental continuity begins with the teacher. A teacher needs to be a specialist in:
- *understanding children*, their growth, development, interests, needs and learning styles, and in understanding each child as an individual
- *understanding the environment* in which children live, not only their physical environment, but that of the culture of their home, neighborhood and community as well
- *understanding curriculum content*, being interested in and knowledgeable about every discipline, with special expertise in at least one subject area
- *understanding the process of planning*, organizing and reorganizing classroom space, schedule and particular content that is appropriate for all the children.

## UNDERSTANDING CHILDREN

In her unit on fall leaves, Consuela illustrated how the expectations of the school are made meaningful to her children. She was able to respond to children's interest in fall leaves and, at the same time, foster achievement of the goals of the school because she knew her children. Consuela's understanding included: 1) knowledge of normal growth and development and 2) understanding of each individual child's developmental level.

## Normal Growth and Development

The universal, predictable sequences of growth and change that occur during the first years of life lead teachers to plan appropriate curriculum that follows children's continuous growth (Bredekamp, 1987, p. 2). With this knowledge, teachers select content that challenges children, but ensures that they will not fail.

■ *Three- and 4-Year-Olds.* Knowing that 3- and 4-year-olds have an extremely high energy level and are refining their gross and fine motor skills, teachers of preschoolers provide for a great deal of active learning. They plan short group times that involve a lot of spontaneous talk and discussion and opportunities to move. Stories and poems that involve children in motion, encourage them to repeat familiar phrases or say the character's words are chosen. For those 3- and 4-year-olds who are ready for longer stories, the teacher plans time when he/she or another adult can read to one, two or even three children, permitting those who lose interest to move to another activity. The teacher selects active songs, in which children are encouraged to move their entire bodies to the rhythm of the words or the music. Children also participate in group rhythm activities.

Centers of interest offer 3- and 4-year-olds opportunity to manipulate their environment, make discoveries about it and satisfy their curiosity. As they work in centers of interest, 3s and 4s are happy to play side-by-side with others, loving and cooperative one minute, bossy and resisting the next. In one preschool, the entire group of 3-year-olds gathered in the block area where roadways were being built. Two or three children would run the cars over the roadway, messing it up, while one child, protesting loudly, spent her time straightening it out. Towers were built and knocked down, and trucks were being driven about, over, under and into things. Children protested others' intrusions, but kept on about their own tasks. On another day, only two of the children used the block area. They built a roadway together, but afterward played with their own cars, up and down the roadway (Seefeldt & Barbour, 1990).

■ *Five- and 6-Year-Olds.* Five- and 6-year-olds are expanding their knowledge of the world and the universe. Their language has grown in terms of vocabulary and the discovery that words can have more than one meaning. While still physically active, 5- and 6-year-olds' bodies are developing rapidly. They are generally quite agile, and now have more control over their bodies. Fine muscle control has developed enough so they can draw representational pictures and can write, though not on the line or in a restricted space. Letters are not uniform, and reversals are still common.

Cognitively, 5- and 6-year-olds are ready to acquire a great many intellectual and academic skills. They become aware that symbols have meaning and that there is a technique for figuring out these symbols. Actual group discussions can take place and children can participate in planning activities. Fives can listen to a visitor, ask questions and summarize what took place during the visit.

Many 6-year-olds are beginning to make relationships between sound and print; by the end of 1st grade they are beginning to read their own writing, that of their peers and even unfamiliar text. Stories can be read together as a group and then reread silently, to each other or to an adult. Children can write stories using their

48

own forms of spelling, grammar and punctuation.

As their social interaction skills develop, 5- and 6-year-olds form friendships and are able to move in and out of small groups. Usually they are cooperative and helpful, and they can assume responsibility for small tasks to maintain both their homes and classrooms. Five-year-olds are beginning to express their feelings in socially accepted ways, expanding their understanding of the emotions they are experiencing and able to attach words to express them. Six-year-olds, on the other hand, may have turned into children in emotional ferment, capable of wild outbursts of joy and sudden shifts to tears. Beginning to be aware of their emotions, they are sometimes alarmed and puzzled by the conflicting feelings they have.

■ *Seven- to 9-Year-Olds.* In the later primary years, between 7 and 9 years of age, children are expanding their horizons. They are still asking for help or advice, but sometimes refuse to accept it when it's contrary to the peer group. Continuing to be curious about their world, they are able to enter into adult-like conversations at times.

By age 7, most children will be successful in reading simple text, and some will be well on their way to figuring out how to decode text and derive meaning. Still, opportunities need to be provided for those children who cannot yet read and ways found to help them discover the process of decoding text and build on their understanding of sound/letter relationships.

Children's written stories become more elaborate as they explore more sophisticated social studies, science and math concepts. They can revise their writing to improve their ideas, spelling and grammar, if such tasks are introduced gradually and with direction and purpose.

Many 8- and 9-year-olds are moving from preoperational thought to concrete operations. They hypothesize and figure out complex relationships. They sustain interest in projects over several weeks. Most children understand how characters in a story change because of the events, though time frameworks within a story may still be difficult for some children. Peer relationships are important and, if they have had prior experiences working in groups, most can function in group projects with minimal supervision. Eights and 9s can take on more responsibility for their own learning and should be given opportunities to make decisions about how to do things and to see the consequences of those decisions.

## Using Knowledge of Normal Growth and Development

Preschool and primary children, so young, so new to this earth, are just beginning a lifetime of learning. They do not need to learn everything during their preschool and primary school experiences. Continually, teachers remind themselves that meaningful curriculum is age-appropriate. When curriculum is inappropriate, the result for children is confusion that often leads to misconceptions.

For example, in one 5-year-old group several of the children's families had new babies. Two mothers brought their babies to visit the class. The teacher read books on birth and growth. The children were fascinated and much interest was expressed in the books and in relating how the real babies were like the babies in the stories. Then the teacher used a strategy that she had heard about from a friend who teaches high school. Following the visit of the babies, the teacher presented each child with a raw egg; half of the eggs had a blue dot on them and the other a pink dot. She explained to the children that they were to take care of their eggs all day, just as mothers and fathers take care of their babies all day: "Babies need a lot of care. It's a big responsibility to care for a baby. This egg is like your baby. If you desert it, the baby may be hurt." The rest of the day was a disaster.

The children went off to work in centers, carrying their eggs. A group building with blocks soon tired of the eggs and put them in their cubbies. Later, much to the dismay of the children, many discovered their eggs had broken. Some children had forgotten the eggs were there and shoved other things into the cubbies. A visitor asked one girl, who was seated alone at a table, what she was doing, and she said, "I don't know, but I know it takes a lot of eggs to make a baby."

After the morning was over and the mess cleaned up, the teacher was asked why she selected this particular activity for the children. She explained that she thought this strategy would teach her students how much care babies require. Clearly, this activity was far too abstract for young children.

The curriculum in this classroom on that day was meaningless to the children because the content was age-inappropriate. The young 5-year-olds, still needing the care of adults, are only beginning to understand how they can care and thus be responsible for someone else. Helping them design a schedule for feeding the class-room animal would be a more age-appropriate way of teaching them this concept. Certainly, the children didn't have the cognitive maturity to understand that an egg represented, or was a symbol for, a real baby.

Activities that are too simplistic can be equally disastrous, resulting in horseplay and wasted classroom time. In one primary class of 8-year-olds, for example, the teacher spread shaving cream on the tabletops and directed the children to practice cursive writing with their fingertips. "Everyone write 'The cat in the hat is on the mat' in your shaving cream," the teacher directed. The children messed around for a minute or two and then began to spread cream on one another. When students were asked why they had shaving cream to write in, one of the children said, "Oh, Ms. Smith thinks we have to feel everything."

Feeling the movement of cursive writing in shaving cream was a meaningless experience for these 8-year-olds. Had they been introduced to writing in shaving cream at age 6, the activity might have had meaning. For 8-year-olds, however, who want and need to be challenged, and who are interested in perfecting skills, writing in shaving cream was age-inappropriate.

To check whether an activity or content is age-appropriate, Spodek (1977) suggested teachers might ask themselves the following questions:

1) Why is this activity, content, experience worthwhile?
2) Why is it important now?
3) Would children gain this skill or learn this concept with ease and efficiency if presented to them later in their schooling?
4) What prior knowledge do children need to master this?
5) Does this offer children a challenge, but a challenge they can successfully meet?

■ *Children's Interests.* Using children's interests as a guide, teachers are better able to select, plan and implement curriculum that has meaning to children. Research shows that when children, as all humans, are interested in something, learning not only has more meaning, but it is more efficient. "Interest-based activities (whether playing with a toy or reading on a topic of interest) are seen as highly motivating and involve attention, concentration, persistence, increased knowledge, and value" (Hidi, 1990, p. 554).

Of course, children are interested in learning about themselves, others and all of the things in their world. Many other interests, however, follow patterns of normal growth and development. For example, 4- and 5-year-olds are interested in monsters, or rather in controlling their fear of monsters. Monster play is prevalent.

A teacher from Reggio Emilia in Italy recognized and accepted children's natural interests in monsters, and redirected their play by asking if children knew anything about aliens from outer space. They then began playing space monsters. She further redirected this play by suggesting that the children create the space scene in which typical battles would take place. Children constructed several space vehicles out of cardboard boxes and recycled materials, and previously uninvolved children were invited to assist in the creation of an "outer-space" atmosphere. Within a short time, monster play disappeared as children were faced with new challenges and problems associated with the space project, including how to communicate with an alien being (New, 1990, p. 8).

Six-year-olds, in the stage Erik Erikson called *industry*, are interested in doing, building and constructing. A teacher of 6-year-olds arranged for the children to build their own playhouse. She initiated the project by introducing children to woodworking. Introducing one tool at a time, she gave the children time to practice with the tools and gain control over the materials. After children became proficient, she suggested that they could build a playhouse that would permit them to carry out many of their play themes out-of-doors.

Together the group met with carpenters who helped them draw up plans. Committees of children were organized to determine what materials would be necessary and how much these would cost. Other committees were created for fund-raising and for trips to the hardware store to purchase the materials. Work started and children were engaged in constant measuring and remeasuring. Finally, the house was completed. Because the children had read materials, written plans, and raised and counted money, many of the school's objectives for children's achievement in language arts, mathematics, social studies and economics were also successfully met.

Another teacher of 6-year-olds rejected an invitation to attend a magic show on the grounds that her children, still in the preoperational period of thought, would not be impressed by magic. She was right. The preoperational child sees nothing magical about a bunny appearing out of a hat and disappearing again. To the young child's way of thinking, the world is full of such surprises. So the teacher substituted a trip to a nearby park to feed the ducks, a very age-appropriate choice for her group.

Knowing that 7-year-olds are interested in collecting things, another teacher arranged a number of ways children could build collections. She provided children with scrapbooks, boxes with dividers, clear plastic containers, egg cartons and a variety of other containers. When the Boy Scouts held a stamp show, she made plans for the children to visit. Fascinated with the idea of collecting stamps, the children explored the role of government agencies in the mail, and the nature of the postal system. Children used mapping skills to locate nations on a globe. Art appreciation skills were developed as children first examined stamp designs from different countries, then created a special stamp for their class.

Eight- and 9-year-olds want to be independent. Teachers of 3rd and 4th grades give their students the opportunity to make their own plans for parties, excursions into the community and group projects.

For example, a group of 3rd-graders, echoing their parents' concern about trick-ortreating, suggested that they might put on a special show for the school on Hallow-een and plan a party for the other primary age children. With the teacher's help, the class decided to re-create "The Twelve Days of Christmas" into the "The Thirteen Days of Halloween." The entire class worked together to re-create the poem, decid-ing on each verse and compromising when ideas were in conflict.

The class at first considered making costumes and being actors, but soon rejected the idea; they decided that they, not the parents, were to be the creators of the entire production. The idea of a puppet show appealed to them. Children in small groups took responsibility for creating puppet characters for each verse. They checked arts and crafts books and sought advice from art and music teachers, as well as parents. They made modifications in their plans and used problem-solving strategies as well. In one instance, when it was discovered that 12 skeletons were going to be too difficult and time consuming to make, they changed words in the verses to one skeleton and 12 ghosts. Lighting, scenery, music, assignment of parts and rehearsal decisions about the show were planned by small groups, but received final approval from the entire class. The class planned and made refreshments and issued invita-tions to other classes.

This does not mean, of course, that every project in a developmental program is a whole group endeavor. Individual children have their own interests and these too should be respected and nurtured. One teacher noticed that two girls were con-stantly bringing her bits of things they had found either in the classroom or on the play yard that were decaying or moldy. In great excitement, they brought her a piece of bread covered with greenish mold. On another day, they spent a great deal of time playing with a can of paint that had spoiled and begun to mold.

Taking her cues from the two girls, the teacher found several books on molds for them to read. She provided them with magnifying glasses to better explore molds and planned a special field trip for them to visit a scientist in a laboratory. To help the girls summarize their experiences, she asked them to report to the total group and plan an exhibit on molds for the classroom. Although the other children didn't become as involved, the exhibits held a special attraction for several children and the girls became "experts" who responded to their classmates' curiosity and visitors' questions.

■ *Progressive Growth.* Children's growth is progressive, sequential and hierar-chical. Children's maturational interests, needs, abilities and inabilities continually change, becoming more complex, sophisticated and mature as they age. Because children's growth is hierarchical, meaningful curriculum will be progressive. Across the preschool and primary grades, progression is built into the curriculum when the teacher "closely observes and analyzes children, then offers materials and activities which provide possibilities for extension of current interests and capabilities" (Ortiz & Loughlin, 1980, p. 3).

Consuela's unit on fall leaves can be extended next year by asking the children to group leaves by their arrangement on trees. Are the leaves on the trees alternate, opposite, linear, haphazard, parallel or paired patterns? Perhaps they might observe and categorize leaves by the nature of their net veins. Children's questions about leaves should be encouraged and ways of answering them explored. For example, in one 2nd-grade class where children were measuring various objects with different units, one child posed the problem of measuring the area of such irregular objects as leaves. Working in groups, children measured the perimeters of several leaves with different devices and then graphed the results.

As children study about the trees from which these leaves come, more sophisticated questions about conservation can be explored: the nature of soil required by different trees, the kinds of trees growing in different parts of the world and contributions of trees to the ecology.

With each extension, more complexity and abstraction can be added. By the time children complete 3rd grade, even though they still rely on their immediate environments as the primary source of data, they begin to realize that their knowledge of trees can be expanded through books, other media and listening to experts.

■ *Individual Patterns of Growth.* Despite the fact that all children progress through the same stages of growth, each is an individual personality with a unique pattern and timing of growth, learning style and family background (Bredekamp, 1987, p. 2). When teachers account for these different patterns of growth in their planning, they ensure that children have meaningful curriculum.

Continuous observation of children and personal interactions with individual children permit teachers to develop an understanding of each child as an individual. Teachers not only observe children, but also talk with them, their parents and their former teachers and visit in their homes, communities and former classes. They thus gain greater understanding of each child's abilities, experiences, interests, developmental levels, and ways of viewing and organizing knowledge.

Many different patterns of learning behaviors and interests are manifested in any one classroom. Some classrooms have a wider range of differences than others. Physically handicapped children, children whose home language is not English and children with learning disabilities are all in regular classroom settings. These children's needs and interests must also be considered in planning developmentally appropriate curriculum. Activities, classroom arrangements and schedules must be organized so that the teacher has time for observing and interacting with children on an individual basis.

The child who is unable to stay on a task, but flits from activity to activity, must have encouragement and support in trying to focus for a bit longer each day. The child who gets stuck on a task and can't let go, making little progress, may need a teacher's help to find the courage to try something new. Some children will learn new skills as they observe, try out activities or interact with others. Other children will need more direct modeling or more structure to their instruction. Devising a curriculum that responds to individual children's needs and interests requires a teacher who can motivate those not interested in the topic and can provide alternative opportunities for similar skills to be learned.

Children can and do learn from each other. Grouping children so that optimal benefits can be accrued by all is a skill. Choices for partners, as well as carefully teacher-selected groups, assist in providing for individual interests and abilities.

The experience of two 1st-graders helps to illustrate this point. Antoinette selected Tommy to work with her on a geography project. She was learning English and found that she could ask Tommy what a word meant without being ridiculed. He always tried to explain and was patient with her when she tried out the word again and again to see if it worked in new situations. He even praised her sometimes and told Mrs. K what she had learned. Tommy benefited as well, for he developed greater skill in explanation and often questioned himself about what something meant and how he knew it.

Permitting some children, at times, to work individually on a project can be the solution for their growth. But knowing when to pull back and require group work may also be necessary. No one wanted to work with Susan because she was so bossy. Being permitted to work by herself pleased Susan, who was making great strides on her part of the "road construction project." When the time came to join the group to put the work together, however, she wasn't willing to compromise her ideas. In a private interview with Susan, the teacher concluded with her that she needed more experiences working with other children. Moreover, one of the goals of this 3rd-grade classroom was learning to work cooperatively, and Susan was not progressing adequately toward this objective.

Susan agreed to try some projects with others, if she could always choose her partners. They struck a compromise. Susan's teacher agreed to start with a support-ive partner, but said that at other times he would expect her to try her hand at working with someone he selected. Gradually, by the end of the year, this 3rd-grader was better equipped to move into 4th grade where she would be expected to do many group projects.

## KNOWLEDGE OF THE ENVIRONMENT

**"** You know," Consuela continues to Claudia, "I think of curriculum as a dynamic thing. I really do base what I do on the goals and objectives of my school system. But how the children achieve these depends on their interests, maturational needs and their culture. Because I want children to be active learners, I also look to their neighborhood and community as I make plans. **"**

Each community has its own characteristics and these characteristics can be used to add meaning to the curriculum. Walks through the children's neighborhoods give one an idea of the community's racial, socioeconomic and cultural components. Avail-able resources are identified, but most important, an understanding of the child comes from an understanding of the environment in which the child lives.

Lucy Sprague Mitchell (1934) explained it this way: "It is the school's job to begin with the children's own environment, whatever and where ever it may be. The complications of the surrounding culture, instead of making this attack impossible, make it imperative" (Mitchell, 1934, p. 16). The role of the teacher, she continued, "is therefore to study relations in the environment into which children are born and to watch the children's behavior in their environment, to note when and how they first discover relations and what they are. On the basis of these findings, each school will make its own curriculum for small children" (p. 12).

In a program based on the notion of developmental continuity, the traditions and life view of the child's community and culture are understood and respected. For example, a teacher on the Navajo reservation who understood something of the traditions and cultural viewpoint of children and their families did not select the topic "Bones" as a curriculum experience, even though it was included in the guide-lines (Ortiz & Loughlin, 1980, p. 11). In the Navajo culture, talking about and han-dling bones are considered inappropriate behaviors.

Visits to the local library can reveal information about the location of the community's special features: parks, museums, zoos, recreational areas, shopping plazas, business districts, industrial areas, churches and transportation depots. The library can also provide details of the community's topology and ecology.

In an effort to provide a developmentally continuous classroom environment, teachers visit places of interest in the community to talk with the people about the services they provide. These experiences help one to build a sense of the community and at the same time make one aware of its resources. Content from curriculum guide units or class-selected themes makes more sense to children when the resources are familiar. Starting lessons with materials from children's immediate environment helps them to discover and explore additional resources in their own community.

Every community has natural resources, people resources and material resources. Becoming better acquainted with these means teachers become collectors of ideas and materials. They get some answers to questions like: What materials can I get free from commercial establishments? What places in the area would be good for a field trip? Which people would be useful visitors to the classroom?

Teachers also collect information about children's background of experience. What knowledge or materials do children pick up when they play in the community? What trees, flowers and insects are children likely to notice? Are there shop windows to look at on the way to school? Are there signs to read? Smells to notice? Sounds besides those of traffic? Knowing about the community, with its sights, sounds and smells, will help teachers plan a curriculum that builds on children's prior knowledge and experiences.

Knowledge of children's environment extends beyond the immediate "here-and-now." Today children are bombarded with all types of information from television, videos, radio, magazines, movies and from the adults who care for them and love them.

Two-year-old Jack snuggled next to his mother, Judy, and listened as she read him poems from an anthology of animal poems. He stopped her and, pointing to a picture of a whale, said, "Oh, oh, bad whale, bad whale." Judy asked, "Jack, why is the whale bad?" Jack replied, "Whale didn't go home. He stuck in the ice." Whales marooned in the ice off Point Barrow, Alaska, seen over and over on television one winter, were a part of Jack's environment. The meaning to Jack, however, had nothing to do with where the whales were, how big they were, or their certain fate, but rather with the fact that they—just as he—needed to be safe in their own home and secure with their families.

## CURRICULUM CONTENT

Meaningfulness must also extend to content. Whatever is presented to young children must have integrity in terms of content. Content is just as whole and continuous as children's growth and development. Just as children cannot be separated into segments for social, emotional, physical or intellectual development, so content cannot be presented as separate and discrete subject matter. Themes or units of study emphasizing key or major concepts have long been suggested as a unifying approach to curriculum.

The idea of key concepts has also been suggested as a way of creating a whole and continuous curriculum. Nearly every discipline has identified the key concepts or scope of knowledge that comprises content. Key concepts can organize discrete subject matter for the teacher. Mitchell (1934) described how key concepts from the field of geography could unify geography curriculum that was once presented to children as separate facts.

Starting with infancy and ending with the 12-year-old, Mitchell specified the interests, drives, orientation and tools of children, and matched these with key content from geography. She observed how the infant, long before walking and talking, attends to and experiences the qualities of things and how the understanding of the relationship of self to not-self develops. The tools of the infant were the use of the senses and muscles in direct exploration. The content of geography was that of directly experiencing the immediate environment (Mitchell, 1934, pp. 18-21).

Jerome Bruner (1966) further articulated this idea. In *Toward a Theory of Instruction*, he pointed out that each subject, each discipline, has its own structure. This structure, based on key concepts, is used by teachers to organize and direct interactions with children.

Others, too, thought that if you could identify the big idea, or the organizational idea of a subject matter, then that subject could be taught to children with integrity. British educators wrote a series of science books called *Science 5/13*. In *Change* (Schools Council, 1973), these educators demonstrated how the concept of energy could be introduced to very young children. They defined the key idea of energy as "if material things are changed, energy is involved." The most elementary aspects of this concept are listed, as well as the specific knowledge and minor and major generalizations of the concept. For example, a specific concept is that "there are a number of forms of energy which are likely to be met with in everyday life," and an example of a major generalization or concept is "many uses of energy" (p. 15).

Currently, content is identified through the use of key concepts. Every field—art, music, science, language arts—has a list of concepts considered key. In the field of social studies, geographers list place, location, region, human movement and environmental interaction, and map and globe reading as key concepts and skills in the field of geography. Economists list the concepts of scarcity, production and consumption, work and exchange, and decision-making as critical to their field. Historians suggest that time, change, continuity of life, and the past are those key to their field. The field of mathematics lists nine key concepts as the content of mathematics: number sense and numeration, estimation, concepts of whole number operations, whole number computation, fractions and decimals, geometry and spatial sense, measurement, statistics and probability, and patterns and relationships.

Knowledge of young children and their environment, coupled with knowledge of key concepts from all content areas, leads teachers to ask:

- *From this body of knowledge and subject matter, what holds meaning for this group of children and for each individual child?* The key concepts of any subject matter are developed gradually, and children will have many experiences with similar materials and content as they develop deeper understandings. How these materials are used depends on children's level of understanding and interests. For concepts related to measurement, preschoolers would be interested in sifting sand and pouring it from one container to another, but a group of 2nd-graders would get involved in weighing containers of sand to determine which one holds the most.

- *What aspects of this concept or content can be introduced to children through their own firsthand classroom experiences or through community field experiences?* Many events in the classroom allow children to expand their knowledge of a subject, but field trips can extend this understanding. The children working on the mold experience were able to read about molds in the classroom and even try some simple experiments. Visiting a research scientist in her laboratory helped these children to appreciate the usefulness of molds.

■ *What ideas or understanding do children have of this content?* Young children's inability to articulate, define or describe a concept does not mean they have no knowledge or understanding of it. For example, children do cooperate, yet few 6- or 7-year-olds can define cooperative behavior. Six- and 7-year-olds do draw maps and can use them to find a hidden treasure at a birthday party, but will not be able to use and understand the abstract concepts involved in mapping, such as scale dimension or key for map interpretation, until after 11 or 12 years of age.

■ *How can this concept or context be integrated with what children have already experienced or learned in the preschool, kindergarten or previous grade?* Children in one school in a port city visited the harbor each year. Preschoolers watched the boats dock and got a short ride around the harbor. In successive years, their teachers would ask what they remembered of the harbor and set up specific things to investigate. By 3rd grade, these children had investigated such things as: types of ships using the harbor, products brought into the harbor and jobs related to the harbor.

■ *What elements of this specific concept does a novice learner need to learn now?* In other words, teachers must differentiate between what a young child knows, understands or discovers about a subject and what the competent, proficient or expert learner knows.

## PROCESS OF PLANNING

❝ I really appreciate your ideas and you've given me some very good guidelines to follow, but without the curriculum guides to follow how do you know what to do?" queries Claudia.

"Well, it is a continual process of thinking and planning," Consuela responds. "I operate my classroom by establishing an overall schedule that is flexible enough so that I can reorganize the children's day, if interests and projects require extended time periods. I call these periods workshops. During these workshop times, the children may be working in small groups or individually. Before and after each session, I usually plan plenty of time for total group sharing and processing of ideas. I also have a framework of skills from the different disciplines that children should be acquiring. These skills as well as themes and unit suggestions come from the curriculum guides. Beyond that I try to be flexible enough so I can respond to children's interests and needs."

Then Consuela adds, "Perhaps it might help if I took you through the process that I am going through right now to extend the children's interest in leaves to a study about trees.

"First, I've been checking the curriculum guides to see if there are some important themes that I should be focusing on. Something I found that lends itself greatly to a study about trees is environmental issues. Children are concerned about what effect events have on their lives, and certainly environment affects them. So, an overriding question for this study will be, 'What effects do trees have on our lives?'

"When planning, I usually try to think of some important concepts and skills that children would learn from such a study. I will also check with the children as we begin the study on what they know about trees and other things they would like to know or could find out.

"Presently in reading we are focusing on 'setting' and in social studies on 'mapping.' I am looking at books and checking on materials to see if this study of environmental issues can be integrated into the skills the children are developing in these areas of the curriculum.

"One of my greatest sources for ideas is the wonderful children's books available. In my search, I found Peter Parnall's (1987) *The Apple Tree*. Since one of the children brought in a leaf from that marvelous old apple tree on the edge of the school yard, I have decided to start the study off with reading that book to the children.

"Although we will add new concepts and probably new skills as our themes develop, some of the concepts, skills and activities that I am going to begin with are described below. **"**

### Study of Trees

Use a small branch of the apple tree in the yard as a stimulus for connecting leaves to their trees. (total group)

Brainstorm with children regarding why trees are important to us and what questions they might have about trees. (total group)

Read Parnall's book *The Apple Tree* to the entire class for general discussion relating to the concepts that children can discover about trees. (total group)

Some possible concepts from the book are that trees:

> provide food
> change during the seasons
> provide joy, delight (aesthetics)
> provide shade and shelter for insects and birds.

Other concepts include:

> Some of the creatures are threatened in the tree.
> Other creatures find protection in the tree.
> This tree grows in a meadow.

Children will select from a wide variety of books on trees during reading workshop time. (small groups or individuals)

In *reading*, children are studying the setting of the story. From reading *The Apple Tree* and other books about trees, they can examine the setting (and thus the kind of environment that trees need). Concepts of setting are:

> Where does the story take place?
> When does the story take place?
> Do time and place change throughout the story?
> Do people or things change with place or time?
> What in the book clues us to the time and place of the story?

In *social studies*, children are studying mapping skills. (total group for developing or modeling the process of doing the activity, and small groups for completing activities)

On global maps, children will locate the places where their stories take place and put identifying stickers with the title of their book on the maps.

Children will make topographical maps and place models of their trees appropriately. This project will require art activities for making three-dimensional tree models (clay, cardboard cutouts, pipe cleaners for trunks, small sticks for branches, colored paper for leaves) and for making a large map with various topographies represented.

Children will create timelines for months or for years using such coding as "In my time," "When Mother was young," "When Grandpa was young," etc. Children whose books reflect passage of time will illustrate on the timeline differences in the trees over the time period.

For *writing*, children regularly keep journals. As they read about trees, they will be encouraged to reflect in their journals: (individuals)

> What is the setting for my book?
>
> What things did I learn about trees from this book?
>
> What would I like to read more about?

Interesting words from their books will be listed, so as they create stories they will have easy access to new words. Those interested will create stories or reports about their trees.

**❝** I believe I have enough material to start this week's project," Consuela reasons. "Some of the presentations or projects will be total class. Others will require children to work in groups or individually. This weekend, as I gather the books for children to read and gather my materials to see how many groups I will have working at one time, I'll decide on group arrangements. For example, probably children will select the books they wish to read and then will be assigned to groups for discussing what they have found out about their trees: where the tree grows, changes the tree undergoes, contributions trees make to our environment.

"As a total group, we will discuss some of the findings and plan out the different projects: topography, timelines, creative stories or reports. Three basic work areas will be prepared, but depending upon the children's discoveries from their reading and their interests, children will select to be a part of one, two or all three activities. The maps, timelines, children's journals and creative stories will provide me information on what students have learned. At the end of most of our units of study, anyway, I ask the children to reflect on what new information or new skill they have acquired. You see, I am trying to get them to become aware of their own learning. **❞**

A curriculum of developmental continuity is carefully thought out. It is developed in conjunction with school or community expectations in mind. Children's universal stages, as well as individual patterns of growth, are accounted for. Curriculum content covers all disciplines—reading, writing, math, social studies, science, art, music, physical education and drama. This content is presented as an integrated curriculum, however, and involves children in active learning. Although children are in charge of their own learning, the teacher is responsible for the content and for providing children a continuity of experiences and opportunities to use both written and oral language to express their understanding and knowledge. Classroom social interactions, important to curriculum development, are provided through shared common experiences, flexible grouping patterns, interactions with the teacher and opportunities for children to reflect upon their learning.

Continuity of curriculum is delivered successfully when the classroom environment reflects the respective growth patterns of the preschool, kindergarten and primary child and takes into account individual differences. Children going abruptly from a play-like, child-oriented environment to an academically and teacher-oriented environment are likely to have difficulty making sense of the content to be learned. Therefore, to ensure early school success, it is important that each classroom setting be geared to children's developmental level and that changes in structure be introduced gradually and on a continuum.

# CHAPTER 5

# *Continuity of Environment*

**"** Helen and I are finding," says Claudia, "that implementing curriculum that responds to children's development takes a different kind of room and more materials than we have right now. Do you have a floor plan, Consuela, that I can use to help us as we rearrange our rooms?"

"No," replies Consuela. "There isn't any one way to arrange the room, and room arrangement keeps on changing. I've rearranged my room several times just this semester. **"**

With the curriculum responding to each group of children, and to individuals within the group, no one formula exists for selecting and arranging equipment and materials within any space or room. It is believed, however, that how the environment is arranged will communicate to children, their parents and others in the school the teacher's expectations for children's learning. The physical environment can communicate to children that they are expected to be socially, physically and intellectually active or that they are going to be passive recipients of someone else's knowledge. It can invite children to give free rein to their intellectual curiosity, or inhibit their need to discover and learn.

Because children under 7 or 8 learn through activity, each classroom will challenge children to intellectual, physical, social and mental activity. Classrooms arranged with centers of interest—learning or activity centers—give children spaces to learn with groups or by themselves, and the materials necessary for active learning. The arranged environment becomes another teacher, challenging children to think, motivating them to explore and enticing them to find out.

## PHYSICAL ENVIRONMENT

Each classroom is arranged to invite children to explore, experiment, ask questions and seek answers from adults, peers and a variety of print, audio, graphic and audiovisual resources. The environment should also be structured in a way that fosters expression. Children's own musings and creative energies are a rich resource for learning. Whether in a preschool or one of the primary grades, the classroom will have:

AN INVITATION TO EXPLORE
From print and other graphic materials
From a variety of audiovisual or tactile materials
With adults
With peers
With one's own inner resources

FLEXIBILITY OF WORKING SPACES FOR
Individuals
Small group activity
Total group activity

SPACES FOR PROJECTS/CONTENT LEARNING
Science
Writing
Reading
Social Studies
Mathematics
Art
Music
Drama
Movement/Physical Activity

AREAS
Creative Arts
(painting, drawing, modeling, writing, designing)
Crafts
Construction
(woodworking, blocks, sand table, water table, creations)
Dramatic Arts
(housekeeping/office/etc., stage area, costumes/props, puppetry, flannel board)
Music/Movement
(musical instruments, record players, tape recorder, props)
Manipulatives
Cooking

FURNITURE
Tables
Chairs
Bookcases
Shelves
Filing cabinets
Sofa
Pillows
Rugs

STORAGE AREAS
Easily accessible for children
(organized so that supplies can be kept orderly and of continued interest to children)
For children's belongings
For teacher's materials
For materials children need permission or assistance to use

## Similar Yet Different

Classrooms across the preschool and primary grades will be similar in many respects. They will also differ, however. A program that provides for developmental continuity will be one in which the spaces for children's learning and the materials within these spaces change often to match children's continuous development.

Spaces may be conceptualized on a continuum: from the simple to the complex, from adult supervised to child supervised, from concrete to abstract, and from those requiring few skills to those utilizing refined, complicated skills.

■ *Spaces Become Increasingly Complex.* Classrooms designed for developmental continuity recognize children's growing cognitive, physical and social skills. Materials in the centers and spaces within the rooms become more complex throughout the preschool and primary grades.

An art center with easels and paints, smocks and paper offers a good example of how spaces become increasingly complex. A preschool setting may have an easel containing only three or four different color paints, large brushes and one kind of paper. As the year progresses in a kindergarten, additional colors of paint and both wide and fine paintbrushes are made available. Although other types of painting opportunities are made available as children become more skilled during the primary years, easel painting continues and a rich variety of colors and types of paints are provided. Textures may be added to paints to enable children to express more complex ideas. In addition to brushes, painting tools such as sponges, tongue depressors and feathers are added. Children also have a large variety of textured and colored papers, cloth, cardboard and wood from which to select.

Children's books provide another example of increasing complexity in use of media. As preschoolers, children use the pictures to enhance understanding of the story, but by 3rd grade the artistic work in children's books serves as models for experimenting with different media.

■ *Spaces Gradually Require More Responsibility.* A program based on developmental continuity is one in which children are expected to use space wisely, productively and responsibly. They are expected to use spaces with increasing independence, such as in their work centers. Three- and 4-year-olds learn to be responsible for selecting the center they will work in. Kindergarten children have the added responsibility of caring for the materials in centers. By the 3rd grade, with limited adult supervision, children should be completely responsible, helping to prepare materials for the centers, caring for them and working independently.

With easel painting, preschool children should have adult help in getting ready to paint and in cleaning up. In 1st grade, children can be expected to mix their own paints. By 2nd grade, they can mix paints to create new colors—chartreuse, pink or magenta—and use a color shell to identify complementary colors and mix other colors. Now children prepare paint sets placed in soft drink 6-pack carrying containers, enabling them to take the paints to another room, the hallway or the play yard when projects need expanded space.

■ *Spaces Move from Concrete to Abstract.* In environments that are responsive to children's cognitive development, classroom spaces and materials become increasingly abstract across the preschool and primary grades. Young children must learn through handling concrete materials. These materials initially are simple, with toys that reflect reality. In the preschool classroom, for example, big blocks and realistic materials related to the children's immediate environment are provided, as children build constructions and enact roles based on their immediate experiences.

Consider, for example, how block play gradually moves from more concrete specific use to more representational use. In kindergarten, large blocks as well as unit blocks extend children's cognitive development. Since objects can now have more than one use, materials from other parts of the classroom are linked to the construction areas. For example: writing materials from the writing center can be used for making signs to name constructions; empty food boxes from the housekeeping area can serve as grocery items in a created grocery store; blankets from the doll's bed can serve as a curtain for the newly designed stage; chairs from the center of the room can serve as seats for the audience.

In primary classrooms, materials useful for multiple purposes are provided. Lego type blocks allow for more complex constructions that children create. All types of ordinary household materials become functional in a classroom committed to children's experimentation and level of maturity. For example, cotton can be used to represent the bunny's tale on a painting, clouds on a diorama or fog at the seashore in a sand construction. Popsicle sticks can serve as a base for a puppet, as building material for a small fort or as a marker on a sand hill to indicate the distance the ball rolled.

■ *Spaces and Materials Demand Ever Greater Skill*. The spaces and materials provided ought to reflect the growing physical and intellectual dexterity of the children. Even within a classroom, spaces and materials must allow for variations. The woodworking table in classrooms for younger children will be different from the one provided for older children. Older children work together with less supervision, so a larger table is provided to accommodate team projects.

In a classroom for 3- and 4-year-olds, children are given instruction and practice in handling one tool at a time, with closer supervision for those having more difficulty. In kindergarten, experienced children can choose to construct an object that requires both hammering and sawing. By 1st grade, children can follow directions for making a construction that requires measuring, sawing, hammering and gluing. By 3rd grade, children who have had these previous experiences can design and then create their own constructions at the woodworking table.

### Arranging Spaces

"Where should I put the library area?" "Do you have a floor plan I can use?" No one way to answer these questions is possible because there is no one right way to plan spaces for developmental continuity. Nor is there any particular formula for selecting and arranging equipment and materials within spaces. Each teacher makes decisions about how to use the available spaces based on knowledge of children's growth and development, an understanding of each individual child, societal expectations and his/her own comfort level.

Thinking about the reality of the physical space, who the children are, the expectations of society, the goals and objectives of the program, and the teacher's comfort level, teachers can solve the dilemma of how best to utilize the physical environment (Seefeldt & Barbour, 1990). Thinking can begin by asking the question, "How can the available spaces best be arranged to respond to children's growth and development and to foster learning?"

■ *Reality of Physical Space*. First, teachers need to realize that some aspects of the classroom are not subject to change. A teacher cannot change the size of the room and where the windows and door are located. Within the space given, however, the teacher can arrange furniture and materials that maximize flexibility for children's social, physical and cognitive activities and find ways to expand the available space.

One teacher began by drawing a floor plan of the classroom, sketching on her plan such things as electrical outlets, a sink with running water, accesses to corridors and the outdoors, storage spaces and built-in shelves. She then asked herself what kind of furniture was available. Which of it could be traded for furniture that could be used more flexibly? She found some tables and small desks, realizing they are easily movable and can be rearranged and regrouped for different projects. Using her drawn plan and looking about the room, she asked herself: What are the safety features that will need to be considered? What is the lighting? What kind of wall space is available? Can work or materials be suspended from the ceiling on pulley-like arrangements, without affecting the lighting or the pleasantness of the spaces?

Next, teachers plan ways to *expand* the space through the use of hallway spaces, other rooms within the building and outdoor spaces. Because learning is not confined to the classroom, the spaces and learning opportunities within the community are considered as well. In considering these extra spaces, however, one needs to ask: Can the corridors be used for group work? Will fire and safety codes be violated? Will other classes be disturbed? How will the flow of traffic be affected? If hall spaces can be used, can these areas be used at all times or just at specific times? Can the work be supervised? Will children be responsible enough to work independently? How will they be supervised in the extra space?

Other rooms and spaces in the building can be found. The media center, the gym or the cafeteria can be used occasionally for special projects, for appropriate individual projects or for total group endeavors. Rules and regulations will need to be established with the children so that productive use of the space is made. The teacher will need to determine if any school rules and regulations govern use of this space.

Even during the winter, children in British Infant Schools regularly use a variety of outdoor spaces for learning. Pets, including a goat the children milked, were useful for direct observation, while living spaces for pets, such as an aviary, were used for both large-scale construction and for measuring activities.

In planning to use outdoor spaces, the teacher can ask: Is the space accessible only through a common door to the building or is there an exit to outdoor space directly from the classroom? Is there outdoor space right next to the classroom that would be used only by one's own class? Is it paved? Is it grassy? Could art, water, sand, certain types of building or experimental projects be safely pursued with minimal supervision? If the outdoor space available is only communal space, what use may I as the classroom teacher have of it?

At some point in planning, the teacher needs also to consider the space in the larger community: learning opportunities for children within a short walk of the school; places where a small group of children with an aide or volunteer parent can collect data for a project (with adequate community support, individual children might be able to pursue a project in the community); business enterprises that are appropriate or are able to assist in expanding children's understanding of their environment; natural environments.

Do all these outside-the-classroom spaces provide opportunities for display of children's work? Can corridor walls be used? Are there display cases? Spaces where projects may be set up? Shops or businesses that would have spaces for displaying children's successes? In some communities, public television stations and public libraries encourage displays of children's work in their public spaces. Some shopping centers also provide opportunities for children's work to be publicly displayed. What criteria should be established for each of the areas for display? What varied opportunities can be found that allow each child to display what he/she does best, or that challenge a child to strive for improvement?

■ *Reality of Who the Children Are.* As teachers plan how to arrange the space available to them, they need to consider the characteristics of the children. This may be difficult, for children change over the summer months and different children may be coming to the school. Still, there are some general characteristics that can be considered ahead of time.

Often the cultural and socioeconomic diversity of prospective children is known. In some cultures, for example, children are expected to share everything and there is little sense of privacy. In others, children may be encouraged to share, but their culture emphasizes private ownership and a sense of personal space. Based on knowledge of the different cultural perspectives of their students, teachers can decide whether they will need to provide more communal space or more personal space to accommodate children's differences. Those children who are accustomed to sharing, with little or no experience with personal ownership, will need space that permits them to learn, share and work together while learning to respect those children who feel possessive about their own space and materials. The latter children will need personal space before they are able to share and work with groups.

The age, maturity, physical development, range of developmental levels and possible interests of the children may be known if these children have been in school before. Check to see if there is a need for desks, tables, chairs of varying heights to accommodate children of different heights. Consider arranging the space so that shorter attention spans can be accommodated, where children who need to move around even while working can do so without disturbing those who may need more private space for concentrating.

Children's previous experiences may be determined from school records or may be temporarily assumed from the environment of the surrounding community. Special space arrangements may need to be made to accommodate children's special interests and talents. For example, live animals can enhance children's learning, but some children may be allergic to furry animals; space for aquariums or terrariums to interest children in fish or plant life would be better. Spaces for cages to accommodate different pets would be more appropriate for children who can be responsible for petting, feeding and caring for them. Some children may be especially interested in artistic development, needing more space and materials for different art media. Consider children's other talents that you could accommodate with special space arrangements.

Howard Gardner (1983) maintains that there are different intelligences, resulting in children having different learning styles. Spaces to accommodate learning through these different intelligences should be provided. In developing linguistic abilities, children need spaces to read, write, tell stories and do word puzzles. For logical-mathematical development, spaces are needed to compute, do experiments and play strategy games. Children with strong spatial intelligence need space to engage in building, creating pictures and images, and designing or "inventing" things. For musically oriented children, space is needed to listen to music, play instruments, sing songs and move rhythmically.

Bodily kinesthetic-oriented children require space to move, to touch and to act out their ideas. Spaces need to be provided that allow them to use their large muscles in jumping, running, climbing and fine motor skills in woodworking, carving, sewing. Children with interpersonal abilities need space where they can work and socialize with others. Children with intrapersonal skills need space where they can work independently (Armstrong, 1987). In providing spaces for different styles and respecting children's differences, the teacher also encourages children to experiment and expand their ways of knowing.

■ *Reality of Societal Expectations.* Often there are school or parental expectations that must be taken into account in planning for space. Both parents and taxpayers are right to expect that children in any classroom show growth and progress toward achieving reading, writing and mathematical skills. Each year children should gain new knowledge about the world around them as they develop problem-solving and creative skills. Children should show progress in developing physical powers, as well as interpersonal and intrapersonal skills.

Teachers should also consider any specific types of expectations for the children in their classrooms. For example, do parents expect phonics and number facts to be learned as precursors to reading and problem-solving? What specific content in science or social studies is deemed important? What is the expectation regarding the role of art, music and movement/physical development in children's lives? What aspects of the children's various cultures are expected to be reinforced? Bowman (1989) suggests that when cultural differences exist between home and school expectations, these discrepancies must be dealt with directly. Thoughtful teachers can assist children in making meaningful connections between their experiences and the new context of schooling.

Space arrangement can partially communicate to parents that these connections are being made as children develop in key areas of the curriculum. Children's previous experiences can be elaborated on in their writings, projects, reading, problem-solving and experiments. These projects should be a part of the classroom decor. Space for these events to occur should be evident through supporting materials in those spaces.

■ *Reality of Goals and Objectives.* Teachers' goals and objectives vary from school to school and classroom to classroom. A classroom organized around continuity of experiences for children must have a teacher whose aim is to nurture growth and learning so that every child remains curious and eager to continue to learn. The rate of acquiring specific skills, attitudes and knowledge remains different for all children as they progress through school.

As space is being planned, the teacher should ask if children will be able to achieve the following goals in the space:

1) Will children show growth in their problem-solving ability? In their comprehension of a variety of printed matter? In their ability to express themselves orally, artistically, musically and in writing?

2) Will their concepts, understanding of and interest in the world about them be expanded? Are children able to become more independent in their work habits and skill development? Are children becoming more skilled at working with a group to accomplish a task and better able to function in a large group? Are they becoming more physically adept and secure in their own abilities?

■ *Reality of Teacher's Own Comfort Level.* Teachers have strengths and limitations that affect how they plan the physical environment. Some questions they might ask are:

1) Is there an easy flow of movement so that I can tolerate the noise level?

2) Are spaces for noisier activities far enough away from quieter activities so children can concentrate?

3) How can I arrange the room so that I will not find it necessary to reprimand children for their more active involvement?

4) Do children have easy access to materials without needing help in getting the materials or in putting them away?

5) Are areas arranged so that appropriate materials may be stored nearby?

6) Are some spaces flexible enough that varying numbers of children may work there, without too much need for rearranging, depending on children's interest and types of activity?

7) Are areas arranged so that I can supervise all the projects, but still have space for assisting individual children or small groups of children?

8) Is the space arranged so that I can feel in charge without having to feel that I control all the activities?

9) Will materials be handy for my use, as well as for the children's?

10) Do I need personal space in the classroom, and will I have some?

### A Case Study: Arranging the Physical Environment

❝ I really don't think a floor plan will help you, Claudia," continues Consuela, "but perhaps it would help if I share with you some of my thinking as I organized for my 2nd-grade classroom to accommodate a developmentally appropriate curriculum.

"This year I changed classrooms and the *first reality* I had to confront was that the *space in the classroom* I was assigned was much too small for all the projects that I envisioned.

"One of the walls had a bank of windows. Although I love all the light streaming into the room, I could clearly see that there wouldn't be sufficient space to display all of the children's work. The first thing I did was to check out ways to expand the space. Two things were in my favor. First, the classroom is at the end of the corridor, so there is a minimum of traffic that goes by. Second, I have an outside door that leads directly onto a courtyard.

"The *second reality* that I confronted was the *maturity of the children*. Could they deal with the *third reality, my expectations and those of the school?* Their teacher from last year indicated there were more mature children who initially would be able to do small group projects with minimal supervision. I was confident that I would be able to organize groups so that more mature peers could assist less mature students in staying on task. By establishing with the children expectations for their behavior both inside and outside the classroom, I will be able to use other spaces later on. Initially I will experiment, using the hall for more individual projects or for occasional small group work, and schedule larger groups when I am confident they will be able to function safely in the corridor.

"Going over my class list, I discovered that a number of different ethnic groups would be represented. It is both a *school goal and parental expectation* that children would share their cultures in various ways, but especially during some of the major holiday seasons. The extra outdoor and corridor space would be important, if I am going to encourage the making of a bower for Seder and a paper dragon for the Chinese New Year.

"Knowing that I would be able to find additional space, I began to arrange the classroom space, keeping in mind the framework. I divided the classroom into four unequal quadrants, allowing for *flexible spacing* for small group, total group and individual activity. Fortunately, shelving was available on all three sides of the room, so the activities that I planned would have space for easily accessed materials.

"One of the larger areas would contain children's desks, clustered in groups of six. Such an arrangement not only saves space, but allows for total group instruction, as well as for small group activities. Desks allow for the flexibility of small group work and for those children who need private space for individual projects. For children who are easily distracted, I can move the desks into a corridor, a corner or use portable carrels. Each child will have an assigned desk that will be his/her private space. Group projects can be done at the clustered desks. A low bookcase will separate the desks from the second large area. A rug will be placed in front of the chalkboard for total group instruction or discussion. The space is sufficient for children to sit in a circle, in rows or in an unstructured manner, depending upon the type of activity. For example, I enjoy reading a story to children at the end of the day. Allowing some of them to stretch out gives a more relaxed and 'enjoyable' atmosphere to the reading.

"Chairs nearby will allow those who need to sit away from others to do so but still be a part of the group. The rug area could also be used by two, possibly three small groups. The bookcase near the rug invites children to select books and read and browse in a relaxed manner on the rug, or to share the book with a companion.

"The third and fourth areas of the classroom will have the activity centers. This year I am starting with a sand table and a woodworking bench, since many of my projects will center around these areas. I will place them in the area of the windows, because there is a wide ledge to display children's creations. Storage shelves will separate the woodworking bench from the desk area. This will allow for writing materials, math manipulatives and games, and art materials to be easily available to the desk areas and for woodworking and construction materials near the bench. A long table will be placed at the end of the woodworking area, providing a surface for many group construction and art activities.

"The sandbox is farther from the sink than I like, but a bucket of water placed under the sand table provides the necessary water for constructions, as well as for rinsing off hands after sand play. I traded my desk, which I never use anyway, for a wonderful round table that fits between the sand table and the rug area. It leaves enough space for a file cabinet that further separates the areas.

"There is also enough room to place two small desks next to the file cabinet. These desks will be available to children who might need more privacy for an activity or for more permanent use. The tape recorder with both music tapes and story tapes will be placed on the filing cabinet and children can use these isolated desks for listening. An outlet is there, just under the chalkboard.

"Since there is not enough space to have a water table or easels permanently placed, I will keep the easel next to the front chalkboard, as a reminder for children's use. When it is needed, it can be moved into the corridor, the courtyard, or with a plastic sheet underneath onto a part of the rug, depending upon the other activities.

"I have been successful in bringing in large tubs for water experiments and rear-ranging the classroom or, if weather permits, taking the activity outside. Many of my water experiments do not require a water table anyway. Sinking and floating experiments can be done in the sink. Examining water from different sources needs only a microscope and bottles. Moving water from one place to another can be done with large milk containers and tubing.

"As I arrange the furniture to meet my requirements, I will walk about the room checking the ease of movement and envisioning the flow of traffic. I will move to different places in the room to make sure I can observe and supervise the children from wherever I might be.

"After making these major decisions, I will review the framework to determine if all major considerations are met. I am quite sure that I have attended to the flexibility of grouping. There are obvious spaces for writing, reading, mathematics, art and for some social studies/science projects using the sand table, water activities and wood-working bench. But you know I will need to consider music, drama and movement.

"Puppetry, flannel boards, boxes with costumes and other props for drama will be stored in the closet. Children will be able to reenact stories from their reading or perform their own creations at the rug area. The outdoor space can be used to practice their performances. Different projects might suggest which prop boxes, flannel board material or puppets I will need to have more readily available for free selection of materials.

"Musical instruments and additional records and tapes will be stored in the closet. The rug area should be sufficient space for learning and practicing songs and for restricted musical movements. For large movement, the outdoor space can be used. There is a music teacher (and room) I will call on for those musical students who need additional support or instruction.

"Cooking will not be an ongoing activity, but a planned one. The shelf beside the sink can serve for the small oven or portable burners, and some things can be taken to the cafeteria to be baked. There are several tables in the classroom where mixing and preparing foods can be done.

"Wall space in the classroom might be a problem. I need enough space to display children's work, as well as for displays that I prepare which invite children to explore, inform them of procedures or answer some of their questions. There is a large chalkboard in front of the room and a large bulletin board at the back of the room. The closet doors near the desks will be used for posting project directions.

"One part of the bulletin board will be used for display of children's papers. Another section can be saved for displaying group discoveries. The tops of the shelves would be available for three-dimensional projects. It would be possible to suspend some projects from the ceiling, but I will ask for a bulletin board outside the room for special displays too. A part of the chalkboard can be designated for children's messages to each other or for safety messages.

"Other spaces for display of children's work can also be arranged. The back of the book display is available; the door into the classroom will be great for a message board for children. Even the sides of my own desk can be useful to display special products. **"**

The arrangement of this 2nd-grade classroom provides children with freedom of movement and materials for exploring similar to those found in kindergarten classrooms. The arrangement also requires children to have more maturity and independence, however, as less well-supervised space is to be used. Materials are of a more complex nature and are organized so that children use them whenever they wish, but in responsible ways. Although children can and do work in many areas of the classroom, desks are expected to be used for some of the projects and assignments. Individual projects and activities are to be pursued, but many will require cooperation reflecting the maturity of the children.

The space allows enough freedom of movement for children to explore, investigate or ask questions of adults and peers, yet it is restricted enough so children learn to cooperate and are not overly intrusive of those who are working independently. The physical environment provides the basis of the social/emotional and intellectual environments. As space and materials are appropriate for different developmental levels, so social/emotional and intellectual expectations should reflect differing levels.

## SOCIAL/EMOTIONAL ENVIRONMENT

Piaget maintains that children are constructors of their own knowledge. If classrooms are to provide environments that foster such pursuit of knowledge, then the social/emotional climate must provide both security and challenge. As children mature, then greater challenges must be available.

The physical arrangement, classroom atmosphere and social interactions can encourage children to explore, to experiment and solve problems, or they can intimidate, discourage testing of one's abilities and limit questioning.

## Physical Arrangements

Whether a room is arranged for a preschool child or a primary age child, the organization of space permits freedom or restricts movement. Rooms organized for exploration have several open space areas with boundaries restricting movement for safety reasons, but allowing natural flow of activity. Although boundaries may suggest different types of activities to be carried on in each area, experimentation requires that space be flexible and that areas have the potential of extending beyond rigid boundaries.

Younger children need more open space as they move about the classroom. Although they are learning the fundamental movements of running, jumping, skipping, hopping and leaping, they do not have such movements under control. Older children still need space arranged for large muscle movements, but they have more control of these movements and should be learning to move adroitly within varying amounts of space.

Children understand what their environment permits them to do from the types of materials available and their organization. When materials are open ended, children know that their vision of how to structure their learning is accepted. Materials that must be used only one way can frustrate children who haven't the interest or skill, or bore children who have mastered their use.

Amount of materials in a classroom can also foster or hinder healthy social development. Young children often can attend to only one or two features at a time. Too many choices of materials or activities can overstimulate or frustrate. Likewise, too few materials can have similar effects. Young children have difficulty sharing or waiting their turn; insufficient materials can result in fighting, squabbling or relying on a teacher to monitor the activity. For older children who are learning to cooperate, only one of each kind of tool in the classroom can force them to figure out a strategy of compromise.

## Classroom Atmosphere

Anyone works better in an atmosphere where individuals are respected, have choices and encounter expectations that are not beyond their ability. Preschool/primary children work best in a climate that allows them to be active learners. They will show their enthusiasm for learning as they move about the classroom and talk to their friends and adults about many things.

Young children are exuberant and often quite noisy. Their talk can be loud as they shout across the room to a friend and annoying as they interrupt peers and adults in their impatience to share. Unrestricted movement and talk do not show respect for others. Children need to learn in a supportive atmosphere how to be active without intruding on another's activity and how to share ideas without always being first.

In a classroom where action is prized and children are expected to explore, conflicts will arise. Young children are egocentric; it is only gradually during their primary years that they begin to understand how someone else feels or that the other person has a different point of view. As children develop, they need to feel secure in expressing their feelings. When children haven't the verbal skills to indicate their frustrations or anger, they resort to physical reactions. Teachers who provide a positive classroom environment devise strategies and use classroom events that help children express their own feelings and understand how someone else might feel.

Having children talk things out, modeling language to use and role-playing their feelings are three useful strategies. Careful observation and knowledge of children can assist teachers in supporting children's growth.

Three-year-old Tian usually showed her displeasure by hitting her companion. Tian's teacher was encouraging her to use words to express her displeasure instead of hitting. At first, Tian's behavior did not seem to change much. Then there was a breakthrough. One day while playing with her friend Joe, Joe accidentally hit Tian's head. Tian looked very startled; Joe looked ready to cry. Fearing retaliation was about to happen, an alert teacher moved to the area and said, "Tian, I think Joe is very sorry. I don't think he meant to hurt you." Tian then replied, "When you hit, it hurts!" "Yes, Tian, it hurts." Tian then turned to Mrs. T and asked, "If I hit *you*, it hurts?" Mrs. T responded, "Why yes, Tian, when you hit anyone it hurts." "Even Joe or my baby?" "Yes, Tian, Joe or your baby." During the day, Tian periodically would ask about hitting other people and it hurting, as if this were new information to her. Tian's behavior began to change. A positive environment, where she could learn how her actions affected others without being rejected, gave Tian the support she needed as she began to realize the consequences of her actions.

### Social Interactions

Young children are egocentric and heteronomous, or other-directed. It is through interactions with their peers that they successfully develop ability to perceive another's point of view and become autonomous or self-directed. Whatever the age of the children, rules for classroom behaviors must be established. Younger children will respond to the rules because an authority figure has established them. They may forget the rule, however, if it hinders them from doing what they wish. Tian knew that she was not supposed to hit, but she continued to do it whenever she didn't get her way. The teacher remained patient with her and used Tian's own experiences of hurting to help her change. Even 3s and 4s can begin to formulate a few simple classroom rules themselves and remind each other when rules are violated.

During the primary years, children take rules literally and begin to accept responsibility for their actions. They are becoming self-directed. When conflicts arise because of different behavior patterns, children can be helped to solve these problems and to formulate their own codes of behaviors. When children are free to do this, not only is their behavior more positive, but they often take responsibility for bringing up and resolving the conflicts.

One group of 2nd-graders was distressed because too much sand from the sandbox was getting on the floor. In a total class meeting, they expressed the problem, brainstormed solutions, experimented with some they thought would work and then reformulated the rules. Primary children do not always come up with sensible solutions and all solutions cannot be tried. Children need guidance in selecting those that are plausible and those that are out of bounds. In a secure emotional climate, children are free to express even absurd ideas without being ridiculed, gradually learning how to focus on more reasonable ones. They learn these skills through experimentation.

Talk is necessary for social interactions. Teachers who insist on quiet classrooms all day long do not provide the opportunity for children to explore how others feel and think. Some teachers believe that children should be free to talk only if they remain on task. A great deal of children's talk while they are engaged in activities, however, is not what one would call "on task." This talk, too, can be productive for learning how to get along with others and resolve conflicts, or for discovering new things.

One group of 3rd-grade children was conducting some experiments at the water table, testing out how to make their homemade sailboats move faster. They were to give a report to the total group at the end of the morning. Josh began to take one of the boats and use it like an airplane. Sandy, a more task-oriented child, became frustrated and went to "tell the teacher." Instead of intervening, the teacher suggested Sandy needed to resolve the conflict with Josh herself.

Upon returning to the group, Sandy asked Josh how they were going to report on which boat went faster if he didn't stop fooling around. Josh figured they couldn't. He put the boat down, saying, "You guys can finish" and went to get a book. The rest of the team members finished their "tests" and were ready for the report. Josh's contribution was to inform the class of the hydroplane boats and the speeds that they could muster—information he gleaned from his reading. He and another child became interested in figuring out how to replicate other boats besides sailboats. Later, others in the class designed other boats and tried to figure out how to give their homemade boats more power.

A classroom where social interactions are encouraged, but where children have the freedom to make choices about their activities, provides much richer experiences for children.

## INTELLECTUAL ENVIRONMENT

An intellectual environment in any classroom assures that all children, as well as the teacher, are learning. Teachers re-create the curriculum with the children. They initiate units and themes that require children to develop math, reading, writing, social studies/science skills. But they build on children's interests, while appealing to their curiosity.

Materials invite exploration and offer choices. The classroom has a variety of materials that may be used in simple or complex ways. A few materials may have one use, but most materials can be used in many different centers and for many different purposes.

As children are encouraged to experiment, so teachers feel comfortable in experimenting. They observe children, reflect on what is happening, pose questions and evaluate their growth. Teachers who provide an intellectual environment, however, also model curiosity and a desire to learn more. They, too, experiment with ideas, testing to see if different materials or conflicting information will challenge children's thinking. As they rejoice in children's learning, teachers share their own enthusiasm for new skills or new information they have acquired.

Children from preschool through primary grades require an environment that takes into account their growing independence. All age classrooms should have physical, social/emotional and intellectual environments that allow for exploration. As teachers arrange space, they take into account the realities of their situations: actual classroom dimensions; age, maturity and culture of the children; goals and expectations of the school and community; and both their and the children's comfort level.

Knowing that classroom arrangements have flexible working spaces, appropriate furniture, adequate storage and display areas frees the teacher to plan for content areas, using a wide variety of constructive and creative materials. The social/emotional and intellectual climates provide the security and challenge that invite children to explore.

# CHAPTER 6

## *Continuity of Evaluation*

❝ It has been a beastly week," exclaims Claudia. "We have been doing standardized testing, and I feel that all the work Helen and I have done to change instruction in our classes is being negated. Consuela, what do you do when you and the children are being evaluated on measures that seem contrary to the goal of meeting children's individual needs?"

"It is frustrating and we still struggle with some parents and administrators who insist on comparing all children to a certain standard whether it is appropriate or not. There's even been some talk about our salary increases being related to increases in children's achievement," replies Consuela.

"So what do you do, give in?" persists Claudia.

"Never," responds Consuela. "We keep plugging away by constantly informing parents and administrators about how the children are really progressing. It is also important to find resources that support our point of view.

"I have found that several national organizations have taken strong stands against standardized testing—Association for Childhood Education International (ACEI), National Association for the Education of Young Children (NAEYC), National Association of State Boards of Education (NASBE) and National Black Child Development Institute (NBCDI). I've shared these position statements with our management team and we've been trying to 'educate' others. I think we are making progress."

"What points do they make?" asks Claudia.

"Well," continues Consuela, "I can't remember everything, but I do know that these organizations have expressed concern that using test results for such things as promotion or entry into kindergarten places undue pressure, not only on children but also on teachers who feel they must prepare kids for the test and thus adopt a curriculum that is not developmentally appropriate. I do remember that Vito Perrone, in the position paper he wrote for ACEI *On Standardized Testing* (ACEI/ Perrone, 1991), called for *all* testing of young children preschool-grade 2 to cease. He claimed that such pressure on kids sets them up for failure and all too often leads to harmful tracking and labeling of children.

"But don't forget, though, if we don't like that kind of testing," continues Consuela, "we have to keep working on an effective evaluation system."

"I can see that. Helen and I are discovering that we really do need better ways of evaluating children and reporting progress to parents," admits Claudia. "It does take time to correct all those papers I give them and to record the results, and all the testing we do really takes a lot of time. But it seems to me that observations, checklists, interviews and work records will take such a long time and I won't have time for the many things we are beginning to do in our classrooms."

"Any evaluation system takes time," concedes Consuela, "but the hardest part is 1) deciding on which techniques to use, 2) finding an organizational system and then 3) communicating to parents and administrators that we have more accurate information about each child's growth and learning. I had to experiment with different ideas before I found what was comfortable for me and for the parents. Now the kindergarten and 1st-grade teachers use similar strategies, and we find we have so much information to share with parents during fall and spring conferences. I'll share with you what we are doing and try to show you some different strategies for kindergarten, then for grade 2. **99**

## A VARIETY OF TECHNIQUES

**66** At our school we use a variety of techniques," says Consuela. "Each is a form of authentic assessment (Kirst, 1991) because each is related to the curriculum and the ongoing activities of the classroom. We found that administering standardized tests took too much time away from teaching. Then, too, the content of the tests, more often than not, was unrelated to what we were studying.

"Some of the techniques we like are observations, checklists, interviews, keeping records of children's work and asking children to evaluate themselves. And, believe it or not, we do use tests. Most of the tests, however, are those I construct. Standardized tests are used for specific diagnostic purposes or for total school evaluations where we test a sample of the students in the school. **99**

### Observations

Observation is an especially useful technique for younger children, but can also be used with older children. Teachers observe informally all of the time, and spontaneously record children's amusing statements, their activities and even behaviors that are cause for concern (Leavitt & Eheart, 1991). Some observations are more formal and planned. Whether formal or informal, observations might focus on:

- whether or not a child realizes there is a problem to be solved
- how children solve problems during play or work, and noting what action the child takes
- what skills the child may need to experience greater success
- children's use of language as they play
- self-help skills, documenting children's increasing ability to dress themselves and take responsibility for their own things
- behaviors during the routines of the school
- use of language observed during reading groups, group discussions or writing activities. Language usage is also observed during math, science, art, music and all other activities of the school.

Observations that will be used as an assessment tool are written. There is no one best way for classroom teachers to observe and record their observations. Early childhood specialists have developed strategies that teachers can try and adapt to their own styles and circumstances (Beatty, 1990; Lindberg & Swedlow, 1976). Many teachers have found it useful to carry a small notebook or note cards in their pockets or on a key hook attached to their belts. Periodically during the day they record, in brief notes, their observations of specific children. To ensure that all children are observed, each day they pick different children as the focus of daily observations.

In order to use these observations effectively and efficiently, the teachers schedule a half hour each day to write brief anecdotes for the children observed that day. They put the observation into a context, describing not only the child's behavior, but when it happened, any pertinent antecedent events, what the child said, the reactions of other children or adults, and how the incident ended.

These anecdotes, often written on cards, are then filed under the child's name in a card file or folder. They serve as useful reminders and evidence of children's development when it is time for more formal reports to parents, or when it may be necessary to analyze and write a narrative report of the child's progress and achievement.

66 This card file is an important source of information for me," says Consuela. "This is the file I go to several times a year before parent conferences or report card time. I take the time to organize each child's notes, noting any patterns of development or learning, content or skills each child has mastered or is trying to master, and those that pose difficulties, and write a progress report on each child. It doesn't take much time, really—not when you consider how useful the information is and the time standardized testing and reporting take. 99

### Checklists
66 Since my school system has as its goals and objectives a list of skills from scope and sequence charts," explains Consuela, "I use this list to form a checklist of 'skills to be worked on' for the children in my classroom each year. I found, however, that the school's list is much too general and long to be useful for my particular class. Each year, after observing each new class of children for about one or two weeks, I begin to tailor my checklist to the particular needs of each year's class. I organize the skills by such things as self-help skills, math skills, reading skills, social skills and physical skills. I list the skills across the top of the paper and the children's names down the side. With the help of the computer, I find I have easily made and personalized checklists from which I arrange the spaces under each skill. When I observe a child performing the skill, I record the date of the observation in the space beside the child's name and make one or two abbreviated notes to remind me of any appropriate data regarding the circumstances. 99

Another strategy that some teachers have found helpful is to generate a set of cards, with each child having a card. As children work on projects, the teacher often notes on a particular child's card what he/she is doing and the date. Periodically, they transfer this information to a checklist of skills to be accomplished. This checklist gives quick information to the teacher about which children or skills have and have not been observed. The objective of reviewing these lists is to prepare activities that will allow children to demonstrate the level of skill they have attained in that area.

With experience, the checklist of skills can be adapted to include math and language skills taken from the board games children play or carefully selected commercial materials children use in the classroom. As children are engaged in their activities, the teacher observes how they use the skills and which they have difficulty with, quickly noting the information on their cards and/or on the checklist of skills.

Children themselves assist in the assessing and eventual recording of their learning. Through individual and class interviews, lists are made of new concepts learned. Older children develop graphs that demonstrate their improvement on any number of different skills. Card files are developed by children in some classrooms to record books read, projects completed or other activities accomplished. With children's assistance, many of these materials, along with the teacher's observational notes, can serve as major sources of information about children's development.

### Interviews

Some teachers have discovered techniques for interviewing children as a means of evaluation. Interviews, so useful in the adult world as people interview for jobs, enroll in college or seek medical help, are just as useful for teachers. A variety of interview techniques can be used. Some interviews take place spontaneously, as teacher and children work and talk together. Others may be more formal.

Informal questions are asked in connection with children's ongoing activities, such as: Why did you put that there? What will happen if . . . ? How many more do you need? When recorded, like observations, these offer a picture of how children are progressing in achieving various skills.

More structured interviews may be useful as well. Asking children a set of questions before and after a unit of work yields a great deal of information about children's learning. Helen Darrow (1964) suggested that teachers ask children questions like: What can you tell me about . . . ? What can you draw or write about . . . ? What can you do to show us about . . . ? Tell all you know about nouns. What do you know about nouns? Show me a noun.

When interviewing children, teachers have the opportunity to probe children's responses by asking additional questions: Why did you say that? How did you get that answer? What might happen if . . . ?

When analyzing interviews, teachers can look for: consistency of children's responses, patterns and logic; consistency of errors; accuracy and completeness of responses.

After a unit on water, 3rd-grade students were asked, "What can you tell me about the water unit?" If the student was hesitant, additional questions were posed, such as, "What went well for you?" or "What did you enjoy the most?" These questions, along with asking for concrete examples of specific learnings and opinions, yielded information for the teacher that was useful in evaluating children's understandings and progress of the unit (Rogers & Stevenson, 1988).

A combination of interviews and drawing tasks was used in one school to probe children's understandings after a project took place. Teachers pasted a sun on each child's paper and asked the children to draw themselves and their shadow in relation to the sun. Before and following a unit on fire safety, kindergarten children were asked to draw what they would do in specific fire situations and then answer questions about their pictures. Using the information gathered from these drawings and statements, teachers were able to assess not only children's growth, but also the usefulness of some of the activities in the unit.

### Work Records

Interviews and observations are wonderful sources of information about children's progress, their strengths and weaknesses, the concepts and skills they have not yet mastered and those they have. Another excellent way of illustrating children's progress is a collection of their work kept over time. Teachers collect all types of work as examples of children's achievement. In many classrooms, children have their own math folders, reading folders, and science or social studies portfolios of projects. Periodically, work samples will be taken from these folders and put into a child's portfolio that is kept by the teacher. These materials are dated and something is recorded about when, how and under what conditions the work was completed. In addition to these samples of children's work, growth charts, photos of children completing skills and tape recordings of their speech can be included in the portfolio.

Teachers skilled in accumulating the data do so in connection with the regular work in their class. Thus it becomes a record that has a combination of all types of authentic assessment.

One kindergarten teacher, Regine, combined her teaching of "key words" into an assessment tool. As children became interested in words and stories, Regine began by having them share words with her that they would like to learn. As they did so, she asked them about letters and their sounds, meaning of the word and its importance to them. She then had them select what they would like to do with their word. For each child, she made a separate sheet on which she kept a record of each word, the letters they recognized, what they knew about the word and how they used the word. She dated each entry.

In addition, as part of her reading/writing program, Regine had children dictate stories about their pictures. She also encouraged them to write. Some children used scribbles, some mock letters, and others letters and numbers written in a string. A few even managed to write their favorite words. At given intervals, she copied and dated samples of these stories and placed them in their portfolios. From these sources, as well as her observation records, she prepared in October, January and May specific information about each child's beginning awareness of the letter/sound relationships, word meaning and language development.

In 2nd grade, Mary collected information in a slightly different manner. Her children were not only writing stories, but were beginning to learn to rewrite stories for "publication." Three times a year, Mary collected one story from each child that included the prewrite, rewrite(s) and final copy. Along with conferences that Mary conducted regarding their story writing, she felt quite confident in sharing with parents or administrators her assessment of each child's growth in the process of writing.

### Self-evaluations

Because it is important to continually encourage children to think about what they are doing and to reflect on their own learning, teachers have developed strategies for involving children in their own evaluation. Self-evaluations help children reflect on and monitor their thinking and learning.

Teachers may give suggestions with checklists, rating scales or other forms for children to complete as they evaluate themselves. Most evaluations, however, will be informal, as children spontaneously discuss what went well, what things they would change and how, what they will want to repeat during the next project and what they will not.

After completing a unit on different land masses, a 3rd-grade class discussed what had been learned. The conversation revealed that the children had acquired important concepts, but that they also had learned important interaction skills.

Pete: "No one knew what a peninsula was when we began, did we?"
Several responses: "I didn't," "Nuh, nuh" and shakes of head.
Pete: "Well, I know. It is surrounded by water."
Jane: "An *island* is surrounded by water."
Tom: "Yeah, Pete, an island is surrounded by water. A peninsula . . . "

Pete: "Well, it has water around it . . . "

Lisa: "What does *surrounded* mean?"

(Silence for a moment.)

Jake, picking up a block and placing it in the center for all to see: "It means that there would be water here, here, here and here." (His hands move around each side of the block.)

Jane, grabbing the block from Jake and pushing it to the wall: "That was an *island*. Now it's a peninsula, 'cause there'd be water here, here and here—land is here."

Teacher: "If an island is surrounded by water, then how would you describe a peninsula?"

Tom: "I started to say a peninsula has water on three sides."

Pete: "And an island has water on four sides."

Susan: "I couldn't say or spell the word *pen-in-su-la*. I first said it like *pensula*, cause it reminded me of Pennsylvania, but Ms. J, you helped me see the "in" in the word. Sometimes you have to look at all the parts of a word to figure it out. I can say it and spell it *p-e-n-i-n-s-u-l-a*."

Teacher: "Good that you remembered that, Susan!"

During this discussion, the children shared what each one had learned, as well as what the entire group had learned. They were reflecting and evaluating their progress.

More self-evaluations take place as teachers ask children to describe their progress in specific curriculum areas. Questions can be asked about literature: What story did you like best and why? Or about art: Which materials do you enjoy painting with? Teachers may also pose questions that call for more general evaluation of the learning process: What did you learn today? What is your best subject? What subjects do you have the most difficulty with? Why? How do you think you can learn to do that? How many things do you know now that you didn't know at the beginning of the year? How many more things do you want to learn before the end of the year?

In one 3rd-grade classroom, children kept book cards of the books they were reading. Some of the children listed those books they read at home, as well. At various times they wrote different information on the card; i.e., characters (list major/minor ones, describe your favorite/least favorite one), setting (does it change), story events and feeling about the book. By using their cards, the teacher could quickly see what books (level, type, number) they were reading and how they were interpreting the story.

After completing social studies and science units, Richard, a 1st-grade teacher, made lists with the children of the concepts they felt they had learned. He posted these lists and at different times asked children to write in their journals what they remembered about a certain topic, as well as any skills they felt they had improved on. The lists served both to jog the children's memories and to aid the children in spelling difficult words. Richard used the children's journal entries to plan follow-up lessons and as references for parent conferences.

These self-evaluations did not tell everything about the classes or individual children's learning, but they did give insights into the agreement between the program's goals and children's expectations for achieving them.

&&  My children are so used to reflecting and evaluating their own learning," concludes Consuela, "it's just a natural part of our work. Children keep their stories in a folder and periodically compare their new story with one they had written in the beginning of the year. They graph the errors they made on their spelling tests and on the 'quick checks' of number fact knowledge. In their journals they reflect about how much better they are able to saw, sew, climb the rope ladder or hit the ball. They keep cards on the books they have read, reorganizing the cards into various categories such as: those I liked and those I didn't like, types of books, books with impressive characters, or by authors. They periodically share with me how they feel about their progress, as did one who was still finding reading a struggle: 'I still can't read as good as Joey, but I did finish two stories that he recommended without any help from anybody this week'. **99**

## Testing

And there are tests. Teacher-constructed tests, especially those related to skill development, can provide useful assessment and evaluation information to children, administrators and parents. When children keep track of their own progress, spelling and number fact tests can even be motivators for additional practice.

A 2nd-grade teacher had a spelling test each week, with a pre- and posttest given. He started off by using rhyming words or words with similar vowel combinations, adding exceptions to rules as children progressed. Children sometimes made up lists of words they would like "to know how to spell this week." As their writing progressed, Mr. D began to use misspelled words from their stories. Children kept their own records of achievement by developing a graph of their *improvement* scores from pretest to posttest. Since the graph named the particular spelling test, Mr. D was able not only to note children's progress in spelling but also to discover what combinations of letter sounds were giving them problems.

With timed number fact tests, children can take the test that best supports and challenges their achievement levels. Teachers can have a series of number fact tests all with the same number of problems. With teacher guidance, each week children select the timed test to be taken. In their math folder, they can keep a graph of the number correct so they can see their own progress. As children develop skill in solving math and other types of problems, tests of various problems can be made. Children can take these tests under varying conditions, such as untimed, timed, solved by myself and solved with a partner. Keeping track of problem-solving progress assists children, as well as the teacher, in understanding how they best approach this learning.

Standardized achievement tests are not recommended for all children before 3rd grade. These types of tests, however, may have a place for some children in a program of developmental continuity. Fundamental to any educational program is the need to assess some children's progress and achievement in relation to other children and to assess the program's effectiveness in relation to local or national norms. Norm-referenced achievement tests can do this. This information, in addition to information collected in the classroom, can give teachers insights for extending the curriculum.

To determine if children in the school are progressing in reasonable ways toward national goals, a random selection of students from one's school can be used. The information can be helpful for reassessing the school's goals.

Nevertheless, achievement tests, regardless of type, only give one piece of information about a given child—how that child stands in relation to the norming group. Many teachers find that this information isn't very useful in planning and implementing curriculum that responds to each child's level; they continue to rely on work samples, observations and interviews, and checklists to help them meet each child's developmental needs.

### Filing System

With all the different types of assessment utilized in a program of developmental continuity, some type of filing system will be required to keep track of children's progress. Different teachers and schools have developed a number of systems.

■ *Notebooks.* The notebook serves a number of useful functions. First, it's an ideal file for organizing samples of children's work, photographs, growth records, anecdotal observations and recorded interviews. Another function is communication. Materials in the notebook are shared with parents during parent/teacher conferences. Filled with evidence of the child's progress in various aspects of the curriculum, the notebook also gives parents a good overview of how learning occurs in the classroom. As parents and teachers review the "evidence," parents are encouraged to add significant photographs, samples of work their child has done at home, or their own observational anecdotes that demonstrate the child's growth in learning during the year. Another function of the notebook is to communicate to individual children their importance to their teachers and parents. Only adults who really care for them would take time to keep a notebook record of important milestones in their lives.

Perhaps most important, however, is the fact that a notebook can go with the child to the next grade or teacher. "In fact," says Consuela, "now that we're in touch with several child care centers, we are encouraging the preschool teachers to use notebooks to record each child's progress. We call that notebook Volume I. In kindergarten, the teacher also uses a notebook and that is Volume II. At the end of this year, children will have Volume III. Since the information is collected and put into the notebooks three times a year, parents can really notice their child's progress."

■ *Portfolios.* Large portfolios or folders are another means that teachers have of collecting and then organizing information used to evaluate children's progress. In each child's folder, samples of children's work, their self-evaluations, photographs or other information can be compiled and analyzed to determine children's growth and progress.

Teachers make decisions about when to sample work that will be collected in the portfolio and how to categorize and judge the work. Some teachers have regular schedules that they follow to sample work; others are more informal. Most try to include samples of work from each part of the curriculum and balance work that is teacher-initiated with work that is child-initiated.

Children and their parents can also select for inclusion in the portfolio work samples or other materials that document achievement. Some teachers have separate sections for child-selected and teacher-selected work.

Portfolios have been used for team parent/teacher/child conferences. In one school, four teams met in a classroom at one time. The child and the parent discussed the child's portfolio, with the child explaining the work that was included and discussing his/her progress. The teacher circulated from one team of parent and child to the other, adding her comments and discussing the child's progress with the parent.

In any case, folios are one way of documenting children's progress throughout a period of time. Showing the parents samples of their child's writing, reading or mathematics work is an important communication tool. Over time, teachers are able to document the progress the child is, or is not, making.

## COMMUNICATING TO OTHERS

**66** I know the kindergarten children are happy," said one principal, "but how in the world can I know what they're learning? I observe their 'published writings,' listen to children read a favorite story and share in the final projects for many children in the school, but I need to have more specific information about what the children are learning. **99**

When teachers change the way educators have traditionally evaluated children's achievement and progress, they also have the responsibility of communicating what their new methods of evaluation mean and how they can be interpreted.

Not all teachers will want to petition the school board to use nontraditional methods of evaluation, as Ann Martin of Brookline, Massachusetts, did, but they will have to find ways of interpreting their methods to others. One 1st-grade teacher involved her principal in her parent conferences. These conferences, which were based heavily on use of organized materials in the child's portfolio, enabled the principal to see and understand the value of nontraditional methods of evaluating children.

Other teachers discuss their techniques in newsletters or at group PTA or parent meetings. Consuela, however, claims communication isn't a problem at all:

**66** Parents love this way of evaluation! They enjoy their child's notebook which has samples of progress in all the areas, and many often ask to look through their child's folders, journals or card files from which materials have been selected. So many have said to me that this is much more useful and revealing than report cards. It is interesting that after a while, fewer and fewer parents are interested in comparing their child with others. They start to focus on the progress their child has made. I even find that many of those 'hard-to-reach' parents enjoy conferences. Since the focus is on progress, they usually leave feeling proud of their children. **99**

Communications with children's former teachers and those who will be instructing them the next year become easier when notebooks or portfolios of children's progress are used. If children are to have instruction that allows them to progress in developmentally appropriate fashion from preschool through the primary grades, then teachers of these different ages will need to discuss children's progress in very concrete terms. Examples of children's work and observations of their activities collected over several years in notebooks, portfolios and on card files can be a starting point for discussing developmentally appropriate practices in joint training sessions or staff meetings the beginning and end of each school year. It is important that teachers, parents and administrators work together to ensure continuity of learning for every child.

**66** As I get better at observing, making quick notes and recording, I find that this method in the long run is no more time consuming than correcting and recording test scores," notes Consuela. "I find that many of my evaluation techniques are also teaching strategies. For example, the children are really learning how to graph, since I have them graph their math skills tests and their spelling tests. Having children write about the concepts that they learned from the 'fastest boat experiment' was a teaching strategy, but it turned out to be a wonderful evaluation technique. Not only did I find out what individual children gained, but I was able to evaluate the unit as well. Besides, it is much more fun, for I learn much more about individual children, their interests and their learning styles. **99**

# *Toward the Future*

  **❝** This year has been an exciting one for me," reveals Claudia to Consuela during their end-of-the-year dinner together. "I wish I could tell you that 'developmental continuity' had been accomplished in my classroom and in my school, but I can't. What I can tell you, though, is that I've learned a lot about children, about myself, about parents and about the community where I teach, because of the changes we've been making to ensure continuity of experiences for our students."

"I did tell you in the beginning that developing strategies whereby all children meet with success in a continuous and developmentally appropriate manner is not accomplished overnight," replies Consuela. "I think what is important is how you feel about the progress you have made in ensuring success for children in your classroom."

"In many ways I do feel really positive," adds Claudia. "Working with Helen, gaining support from my principal, seeing many more parents becoming positively involved with their children's learning means a lot. We don't have a school management team functioning as I would like to see, however. We are meeting resistance from some of the other teachers who find our kids 'too involved and active.' They can't see the organization and structure that's there. I'm afraid that next year they will turn off some children, who are just beginning to develop reading and writing skills, because they will insist on the children doing worksheets."

"Wait a minute!" exclaims Consuela. "It sounds to me like you want a *rev*olution and are maybe too impatient for the *ev*olution to take place."

"You're right," concedes Claudia. "I've become a convert. I have learned that I can make some important changes in my classroom and work with preschool, kindergarten, other primary teachers and parents to make developmental continuity more of a reality for all children. I've made changes in my curriculum, in the organization of my classroom, and I've seen the positive results for so many children. I also recognize that I've missed the boat with some of the children and am anxious to learn what I can do to help them achieve their potential. Then, I just get so impatient. I am pleased that we are being given more authority and are finding resources to make some of the important changes. It's just that I want everyone on board for these changes and that takes lots of time and energy."

"You know that many of the ideas or strategies that relate to developmental continuity have been tried before," says Consuela. "Remember the nongraded schools in our district? In some of the schools the projects met with success, while in others too many children may have initially made good progress only to have met with failure later on. But we must not be discouraged, for ours is a new challenge. It is one that the entire community must embrace. It requires support from everyone if we are to provide an environment where youngsters will be able 'to use their minds well, so they may be prepared for responsible citizenship, further learning, and productive employment in our modern economy' (U.S. Department of Education, 1991, p. 3). **❞**

Indeed, as Consuela notes, the ideas and strategies for developmental continuity have been successfully implemented over the years by good teachers in many schools. Forces within the society have either supported or negated the efforts of these excellent teachers. In many school systems, parents and community service agencies have worked with teachers to provide appropriate learning environments for some children.

A "nation at risk" is not without any success stories. It is a nation, however, where not enough children are receiving the kind of support they need to meet the challenges they will face in an ever-changing and more complex society. The nation has moved from an industrialized society that needed workers for the assembly line to an information society that needs workers who can use their intelligence to solve problems and who can be flexible and adapt to change.

In the past, teachers were entrusted with education of the nation's children. Over time, however, that responsibility has been taken away. Decisions about curriculum have been made by administrators, supervisors and legislators. Too often this policy has resulted in a set curriculum. It was believed that if all teachers followed the same guides, children would acquire the same knowledge and skills. For too many children, the skills and knowledge necessary for continuous growth have not been learned, and rigid curriculum has frustrated and impeded others.

The nation is rediscovering that it is time for educators, parents, legislators and business people to join forces in a concerted effort to ensure the success of all children, using the accumulated knowledge about how different children learn, and to provide schools and homes with the resources needed.

With each attempt to build developmental continuity in children's early educational experiences across the preschool and primary grades, progress was made. Today the opportunity to build on this progress exists. Aware that children do not magically change as they move from the preschool to the kindergarten and primary grades, more and more schools are finding ways to build bridges between children's early educational experiences. Awareness is increasing that today's behavioristic, lock-step curriculum has not only been unsuccessful but has, in fact, been damaging. Parents, teachers, school board members and national leaders have begun to search for more efficient and effective methods of early education.

It is time to assess the successes of these earlier programs that showed how to provide good educational programs for all children and to build on those successes. It is time to recognize that, although children progress through similar stages of development as they move across the preschool and primary grades, this development is not equal or identical. It is time to recognize that children learn best as they are allowed to construct knowledge and that schools—whether child care centers, preschools or public schools—must provide environments that ensure that children's educational experiences will support their growth, development and different modes of learning. It is time to mobilize all those who are concerned about children's education and to include teachers, parents and community support groups in the process of reorganizing schools for developmental continuity.

# Bibliography

**References**

Administration for Children, Youth and Families. (1988). *Easing the transition: From preschool to kindergarten. A guide for early childhood teachers and administrators*. Washington, DC: Administration for Children, Youth and Families and U.S. Department of Health and Human Services.

Armstrong, T. (1987). *In their own way: Discovering and encouraging your child's learning style*. Los Angeles: Jeremy P. Tarcher.

Association for Childhood Education International/Perrone, V. (1991). *On standardized testing: A position paper*. Wheaton, MD: ACEI.

Barbour, N. H. (1990). Flexible grouping: It works! *Childhood Education, 67*, 66-68.

Barbour, N. H., & Seefeldt, C. (1992). Developmental continuity: From preschool through primary grades. *Childhood Education, 68*, 302-304.

Beatty, B. (1989). Child gardening: The teaching of young children in America. In D. Warren (Ed.), *American teachers* (pp. 65-98). New York: Macmillan.

Beatty, J. J. (1990). *Observing development of the young child* (2nd ed.). Columbus, OH: Charles E. Merrill.

Berrueta-Clement, J. (1980). *Assessment of program impact through first grade, Vol. V: Impact on children. An evaluation of Project Developmental Continuity*. Washington, DC: U.S. Department of Health, Education, and Welfare.

Bowman, B. (1989). Educating language-minority children: Challenges and opportunities. *Phi Delta Kappan, 71*, 118-121.

Brandt, R. S. (1989). On parents and schools: A conversation with Joyce Epstein. *Educational Leadership, 47*(2), 24-27.

Bredekamp, S. (1987). *Developmentally appropriate practice in early childhood programs serving children from birth through age 8: Expanded edition*. Washington, DC: National Association for the Education of Young Children.

Bronfenbrenner, U. (1979). *The ecology of human development: Experiments by nature and design*. Cambridge: Harvard University Press.

Bruner, J. (1966). *Toward a theory of instruction*. Cambridge: Harvard University Press.

Cazden, C. B. (1986). Classroom discourse. In M. E. Wittrock (Ed.), *Handbook of research on teaching* (3rd ed.), (pp. 432-464). New York: Macmillan.

Connell, D. R. (1987). The first 30 years were the fairest: Notes from the kindergarten and ungraded primary (K-1-2). *Young Children, 42*(1), 30-39.

Cook, L., Gumperz, J., & Gumperz, B. (1982). Communicative competence in educational perspective. In L. Cherry Wilkenson (Ed.), *Communication in classrooms*. New York: Academic Press.

Darrow, H. (1964). *Research: Children's concepts*. Washington, DC: Association for Childhood Education International.

Dewey, J. (1944). *Democracy and education*. New York: Free Press.

Dyson, A. H. (1987). The value of time off tasks: Young children's spontaneous talk and deliberate text. *Harvard Educational Review, 57*, 534-564.

Eisner, E. W. (1988). The primacy of experience and the politics of method. *Educational Researcher, 17*(5), 15-21.

Flanders, N. A. (1970). *Analyzing teacher behavior*. Reading, MA: Addison Wesley.

Galen, H. (1991). Increasing parent involvement in elementary school: The nitty-gritty of one successful program. *Young Children, 46*(2), 18-28.

Gardner, H. (1983). *Frames of mind: The theory of multiple intelligences*. New York: Basic Books.

Goodlad, J. (1984). *A place called school*. New York: McGraw Hill.

Goodlad, J., & Anderson, R. H. (1959). *The nongraded elementary school*. New York: Teachers College Press.

Heath, S. B. (1983). *Ways with words: Language, life and work in communities and classrooms*. Cambridge, MA: Cambridge University Press.

Heath, S. B., & McLaughlin, M. W. (1989). A child resource policy: Moving beyond dependence on school and family. *Phi Delta Kappan, 68*, 576-581.

Hidi, S. (1990). Interest and its contribution as a mental resource for learning. *Review of Educational Research, 60*, 549-573.

Iran-Nejad, A., McKeachie, W. J., & Berliner, D. C. (1990). The multisource nature of learning: An introduction. *Review of Educational Research, 60*, 509-517.

Karweit, N. (1988). Quality and quantity of learning time in preprimary programs. *The Elementary School Journal, 89*, 119-135.

Katz, L., Evangelou, D., & Hartman, J. A. (1990). *The case for mixed-age grouping in early education.* Washington, DC: National Association for the Education of Young Children.

Kirst, M. W. (1991). Interview on assessment issues with Lorrie Shepard. *Educational Researcher, 20*(2), 21-24.

Krulee, G. K., Hetzner, W. A., & McHenry, E. J. (1973). *An analysis of Project Follow Through: Final report.* Washington, DC: U.S. Department of Health, Education, and Welfare.

Leavitt, R. L., & Eheart, B. K. (1991). Assessment in early childhood programs. *Young Children, 46*(5), 4-10.

Lefrancois, G. R. (1989). *Of children: An introduction to child development* (6th ed.). Belmont, CA: Wadsworth.

Lindberg, L., & Swedlow, R. (1976). *Early childhood education: A guide to observing.* Boston: Allyn & Bacon.

MacDowell, M. A. (1989). Partnerships: Getting a return on the investment. *Educational Leadership, 47*(2), 8-15.

Manning, M. L. (in press). *Developmentally appropriate middle level schools.* Wheaton, MD: Association for Childhood Education International.

Martin, A. (1985). Back to kindergarten basics. *Harvard Educational Review, 55*, 318-321.

Milwaukee Public Schools. (1942). *Curriculum guide for kindergarten-primary.* Milwaukee, WI: Author.

Mitchell, L. S. (1934). *Young geographers.* New York: Bank Street College.

Mitchell, A., & Modigliani, K. (1989). Young children in public schools: The "only ifs" reconsidered. *Young Children, 44*(6), 56-61.

Morine-Dershimer, G., & Tenenberg, M. (1992). *Participant perspectives of classroom discourse.* Final Report Executive Summary (NIE G78-0161). Washington, DC: National Institute of Education.

National Association for the Education of Young Children. (1988). *Testing young children: Concerns and cautions.* Washington, DC: Author.

National Association of Elementary School Principals. (1990). *Early childhood education and the elementary school principal: Standards for quality programs for young children.* Alexandria, VA: Author.

National Association of State Boards of Education. (1988). *Right from the start.* Alexandria, VA: Author.

New Jersey State Department of Education. (1989). *Guide for teachers, parents, and parent coordinators: Planning for parental involvement in early childhood education.* Trenton, NJ: Author.

New, R. (1990). *Early child-care and education, Italian style: The Reggio Emilia daycare and preschool program.* Unpublished paper, University of New Hampshire.

Oberlander, T. M. (1989). A nongraded, multi-age program that works. *Principal, 68*(5), 29-31.

Ortiz, L. I., & Loughlin, C. E. (1980). *Building curriculum with children: A point of view.* Albuquerque, NM: University of New Mexico.

Parker, S., & Temple, A. (1925). *Unified kindergarten and first-grade teaching.* Boston: Ginn.

Parnall, P. (1987). *The apple tree.* New York: Macmillan.

Piaget, J., & Inhelder, B. (1969). *The psychology of the child.* New York: Basic Books.

Powell, D. R. (1990). Home visiting in the early years: Policy and program design decisions. *Young Children, 45*(6), 65-74.

*Project construct: A framework for curriculum and assessment.* (1991). Columbia, MO: University of Missouri and Missouri Department of Elementary and Secondary Education.

Rapoport, R. W. (Ed). (1985). *Children, youth and families: The action research relationship.* Cambridge, MA: Cambridge University Press.

Rogers, V. R., & Stevenson, C. (1988). How do you know what the kids are learning? *Educational Leadership, 45*(5), 68-75.

Schools Council. (1973). *Change. Guide to Science 5/13*. London: Macdonald Educational.

Seefeldt, C., & Barbour, N. H. (1990). *Early childhood education: An introduction* (2nd ed.). Columbus, OH: Charles E. Merrill.

Severn, L. (1992). Cooperation between the school board and the corporate board creates a kindergarten. *Young Children, 47*(4), 62-64.

Shepard, L. A., & Smith, M. L. (1988). Escalating academic demand in kindergarten: Counterproductive policies. *The Elementary School Journal, 89*, 135-147.

Spodek, B. (1977). What constitutes worthwhile educational experiences for young children? In B. Spodek (Ed.), *Teaching practices? Reexamining assumptions* (pp. 332-377). Washington, DC: National Association for the Education for Young Children.

St. Louis Association for the Education of Young Children. (1989). *Early childhood transfer form.* St. Louis, MO: Author.

Stallings, J., & Kaskowitz, D. (1974). *Follow through classroom observation evaluation, 1972-73*. Menlo Park, CA: SRI International.

State of Connecticut. (1988). *A guide to program development for kindergarten.* Hartford, CT: State Department of Education.

U.S. Department of Education. (1974). *Project Developmental Continuity*. Washington, DC: Author.

U.S. Department of Education. (1991). *America 2000. An education strategy*. Washington, DC: Author.

Vandergrift, J. A., & Greene, A. L. (1992). Rethinking parent involvement. *Educational Leadership, 50*(1), 57-59.

Vygotsky, L. (1986). *Thought and language* (rev. ed.). Cambridge: M.I.T. Press.

Walsh, J. D. (1989). Changes in kindergarten: Why here? Why now? *Early Childhood Research Quarterly, 4*, 377-393.

Wiggan, K. D., & Smith, N. A. (1896). *Kindergarten principles and practices.* Boston: Houghton Mifflin.

# *Categorized References*

### Authentic Assessment

Grace, C., & Shores, E. F. (1992). *The portfolio and its use: Developmentally appropriate assessment of young children.* Little Rock, AR: Southern Association for Children Under Six.

Lamme, L. L., & Hysmith, C. (1991). One school's adventure into portfolio assessment. *Language Arts, 68*, 629-640

Linder, T. (1990). *Transdisciplinary play-based assessment.* Baltimore, MD: Brookes Publishing.

Maeroff, G. L. (1991). Assessing alternative assessment. *Phi Delta Kappan, 73*, 272-282.

Meitzel, S. J., & Steele, D. M. (1991). *The early childhood portfolio collection process.* Ann Arbor, MI: Center for Human Growth and Development, University of Michigan.

Shepard, L. A. (1982). *Assessment of learning disabilities.* ERIC Document Reproduction Service No. ED 227 134.

Teale, W. H. (1988). Developmentally appropriate assessment of reading and writing in the early childhood classroom. *The Elementary School Journal, 89*, 173-183.

### British Infant Schools

Murrow, C., & Murrow, L. K. (1971). *Children come first: The inspired work of English primary schools.* New York: American Heritage Press.

Rogers, V. R. (1970). *Teaching in the British primary school.* New York: Macmillan.

Weber, L. (1971). *English Infant School and information education.* Englewood Cliffs, NJ: Prentice Hall.

## Community Involvement (Collaborative Efforts with Other Agencies)

Center for the Future of Children. (1992). *The future of children: School linked services.* Los Altos, CA: Center for the Future of Children and David and Lucile Packard Foundation.

Clark, T. A. (1992). *Collaboration to build competence.* Washington, DC: U.S. Department of Education.

Melavile, A., & Blank, M. (1991). *What it takes: Structuring interagency partnerships to connect children and families with comprehensive services.* Washington, DC: Education and Human Services Consortium.

National Association of State Boards of Education. (1991). *Caring communities: Supporting young children and families.* Alexandria, VA: Author.

U.S. Department of Education. (1992). *America 2000 communities: Getting started.* Washington, DC: Author.

U.S. Department of Health and Human Services. (1991). *Sticking together.* Washington, DC: Author.

## Cooperative Learning

Johnson, D. W., Johnson, R. T., & Johnson-Halubec, E. (1990). *Circles of learning: Cooperation in the classroom* (3rd ed.). Edina, MN: Interaction Book.

Sharan, Y., & Sharan, S. (1992). *Group investigation: Expanding cooperative learning.* New York: Teachers College Press.

Slavin, R. E. (1990). *Cooperative learning: Theory, research, and practice.* Englewood Cliffs, NJ: Prentice Hall.

## Developmentally Appropriate Practice

Beatty, J. J. (1992). *Preschool: Appropriate practices.* New York: Harcourt Brace Jovanovich.

Bredekamp, S. (Ed.). (1987). *Developmentally appropriate practice in early childhood programs serving children from birth through 8.* Washington, DC: National Association for the Education of Young Children.

Fromberg, D. (1992). *The full-day kindergarten.* New York: Teachers College Press.

## Follow Through

Krulee, G. K., Hetzner, W. A., & McHenry, E. J. (1973). *An analysis of Project Follow Through: Final report.* Washington, DC: U.S. Department of Health, Education, and Welfare.

Stallings, J., & Kaskowitz, D. (1974). *Follow through classroom observation evaluation, 1972-73.* Menlo Park, CA: SRI International.

## Froebelian Curriculum (Froebel's Gifts and Occupations)

Lawrence, E. M. (1969). *Froebel and English education: Perspectives on the founder of the kindergarten.* New York: Schocken Books.

## Integrated Curriculum (Project Approach, Teaching Through Themes, Units)

Friedl, A. E. (1986). *Teaching science to children: An integrated approach.* New York: Random House.

Katz, L., & Chard, S. (1989). *Engaging children's minds: The project approach.* Norwood, NJ: Ablex.

Stafford, P. L. (1989). *Integrated teaching in early childhood education. Starting in the mainstream.* White Plains, NY: Longman.

## Language Experience Approach

Allen, R. V., & Allen, C. (1982). *Language experience activities* (2nd ed.). Boston: Houghton Mifflin.

Hall, M. A. (1978). *The language experience approach for teaching reading: A research perspective* (2nd ed.). Urbana, IL: International Reading Association.

Hall, M. A. (1981). *Teaching reading as a language experience* (3rd ed.). Columbus, OH: Charles E. Merrill.

Stauffer, R. G. (1970). *The language experience approach to the teaching of reading.* New York: Harper-Collins.

Veatch, J. (1973). *Key words to reading: The language experience approach begins.* Columbus, OH: Charles E. Merrill.

## Key Concepts

American Association for the Advancement of Science. (1989). *Science for all Americans.* Washington, DC: Author.

Maryland State Department of Education. (n.d.). *English language arts. A Maryland curricula framework.* Baltimore, MD: Author.

National Council for Geographic Education and Association of American Geographers. (1984). *Guidelines for geographic education: Elementary and secondary schools.* Washington, DC: National Council for Geographic Education.

National Council of Teachers of Mathematics: Commission of Standards for School Mathematics. (1989). *Curriculum and evaluation standards for school mathematics.* Reston, VA: Author.

## Multi-age Grouping/Family Groupings

Katz, L., Evangelou, D., & Hartman, J. A. (1990). *The case for mixed-age grouping in early education.* Washington, DC: National Association for the Education of Young Children.

Lodish, R. (1992). The pros and cons of mixed age grouping. *Principal, 71*(6), 20-22.

Surbeck, E. (1992). Multi-age programs in primary grades: Are they educationally appropriate? *Childhood Education, 69*, 3-4.

## Nongraded Elementary School

Connell, D. R. (1987). The first 30 years were the fairest: Notes from the kindergarten and ungraded primary (K-1-2). *Young Children, 42*(1), 30-39.

Goodlad, J. (1984). *A place called school.* New York: McGraw Hill.

Goodlad, J., & Anderson, R. H. (1959). *The nongraded elementary school.* New York: Teachers College Press.

## Parent Involvement

Brandt, R. S. (Ed.). (1989). Strengthening partnerships with parents and community. *Educational Leadership, 47*(2), entire issue.

Galinsky, E., Shinn, M., Phillips, D., Hawes, C., & Whitebook, M. (1990). *Parent teacher relationships.* New York: Families & Work Institute.

Honig, A. (1982). Parent involvement in early childhood education. In B. Spodek (Ed.), *Handbook of research in early childhood education* (pp. 426-456). New York: Free Press.

Kaplan, L. (Ed.). (1992). *Education and the family.* Boston: Allyn & Bacon.

Walker, S. F. (1988). *Drawing in the family.* Denver: Education Commission of the States.

## Piagetian-based Curriculum

DeVries, R., & Kohlberg, L. (1987). *Programs of early childhood education: The constructivist view.* Washington, DC: National Association for the Education of Young Children.

Forman, G., & Kuschner, D. (1983). *The child in construction of knowledge: Piaget for teaching children.* Washington, DC: National Association for the Education of Young Children.

Furth, H. G. (1970). *Piaget for teachers.* Englewood Cliffs, NJ: Prentice Hall.

Peterson, R., & Felton-Collins, V. (1986). *The Piaget handbook for teachers and parents: Children in the age of discovery, preschool-third grade.* New York: Teachers College Press.

## Project Developmental Continuity

Berrueta-Clement, J. (1980). *Assessment of program impact through first grade, Vol. V: Impact on children. An evaluation of Project Developmental Continuity.* Washington, DC: U.S. Department of Health, Education, and Welfare.

U.S. Department of Education. (1974). *Project developmental continuity.* Washington, DC: Author.

## Phonic Skills

Heilman, A. W. (1989). *Phonics in proper perspective* (6th ed.). Columbus, OH: Charles E. Merrill.

## Preoperational Period of Thinking

Ginsberg, H., & Opper, S. O. (1988). *Piaget's theory of intellectual development* (3rd ed.). Englewood Cliffs, NJ: Prentice Hall. (Chap. 3, The years 2 through 11: The semiotic function in Piaget's early work, pp. 69-112; Chap. 4, The years 2 through 11: Piaget's later work, pp. 113-179.)

Piaget, J., & Inhelder, B. (1969). *Psychology of the child* (H. Weaver, Trans.). New York: Basic Books. (Chap. 3, The semiotic or symbolic function, pp. 51-91.)

## Retention/Transitional Classrooms

Delidow, S. V. (1989). *A longitudinal study of retention.* Rascommon, MI: C.O.O.P. Intermediate Board of Education. (ERIC Document Reproduction Service No. ED 303 558)

Egertson, H. A. (1987). *Unacceptable trends in kindergarten entry and placement: A position statement.* Chicago: National Association of Early Childhood Specialists in State Departments of Education. (ERIC Document Reproduction Service No. ED 297 856)

Gredler, G. R. (1984). Transition classes: A viable alternative for the at-risk child. *Psychology in the Schools, 21*, 463-470.

Shepard, L. A., & Smith, M. L. (1986). Synthesis of research on school readiness and kindergarten retention. *Educational Leadership, 44*(3), 78-86.

## Sensorimotor Stages of Development

Ginsberg, H., & Opper, S. O. (1988). *Piaget's theory of intellectual development* (3rd ed.). Englewood Cliffs, NJ: Prentice Hall. (Chap. 2, Infancy sensorimotor period, pp. 26-72.)

Piaget, J., & Inhelder, B. *Psychology of the child* (H. Weaver, Trans.). New York: Basic Books. (Chap. 1, The sensorimotor level, pp 3-28.)

## Standardized Testing

Association of Childhood Education International/Perrone, V. (1991). *On standardized testing: A position paper.* Wheaton, MD: ACEI.

Meisel, S. J. (1987). Uses and abuses of developmental screening and school readiness testing. *Young Children, 42*(2), 4-9.

National Association for the Education of Young Children. (1988). *Position statement on standardized testing of young children 3 through 8 years of age.* Washington, DC.: Author.

Neill, M. D., & Medina, N. J. (1989). Standardized testing: Harmful to educational health. *Phi Delta Kappan, 70*, 688-697.

*Standards for educational and psychological testing.* (1985). Washington, DC: American Psychological Association, American Educational Research Association and National Council on Measurement in Education.

## Transitions from Preschool/Kindergarten to Primary Grades

Lombardi, J. (1992). *Beyond transition: Ensuring continuity in early childhood services.* Urbana, IL: ERIC Clearinghouse on Elementary and Early Childhood Education.

Love, J. M., & Logue, M. E. (1992). *Transitions to kindergarten in American schools.* Washington, DC: U.S. Department of Education.

Seefeldt, C. (1990). *Continuity of curriculum from preschool to the primary grades.* Washington, DC: U.S. Department of Education.

Silvern, S. (1988). Continuity/discontinuity between home and early childhood education environments. *The Elementary School Journal, 89,* 147-159.

Southern Association for Children Under Six. (1990). *Continuity of learning for four-to-seven-year-old children: A position paper.* Little Rock, AR: Author.

U.S. Department of Health and Human Services. (1988). *Easing the transition from preschool to kindergarten.* Washington, DC: Author.

## Whole Language

Goodman, K. S. (1986). *What's whole in whole language?* Portsmouth, NH: Heinemann.

Jewell, M. G., & Zintz, M. V. (1990). *Learning to read and write naturally* (2nd ed.). Dubuque, IA: Kendall/Hunt.

Morrow, L. M. (1989). *Literacy development in the early years.* Englewood Cliffs, NJ: Prentice Hall.

Schickedanz, J. A. (1986). *More than the ABC's. The early stages of reading and writing.* Washington, DC: National Association for the Education of Young Children.

Smith, F. R. (1988). *Understanding reading: A psycholinguistic analysis of reading and learning to read.* Hillsdale, NJ: Erlbaum Associates.

Teale, W. H., & Sulzby, E. (Eds.). (1986). *Emergent literacy: Writing and reading.* Norwood, NJ: Ablex.

# ACEI MEMBERSHIP MAKES SENSE!

**Childhood Education**—Each issue informs and inspires the classroom teacher with cutting-edge articles on innovative classroom practices, current education issues and vital research on childhood education. Each issue of *Childhood Education* includes a 16-page *ACEI Exchange Newsletter*. This special section keeps you up-to-date on Association happenings and local and state ACEI events, and features a pullout section of practical classroom idea sparkers. Published five times annually.

**Annual Study Conference**—The ACEI Conference offers more than 100 exciting professional sessions and workshops. It attracts leading educators from around the world who enjoy lively presentations, educational exhibits and materials and informal exchanges.

**ACEI Divisions**—The ACEI Professional Divisions— Infancy, Early Childhood and Later Childhood/Early Adolescence—address members' interests in specific developmental stages. Each Division publishes a quarterly newsletter. Only ACEI Members are eligible to join ACEI Divisions.

**ACEI State Associations and Local Branches**—ACEI Members value the special camaraderie of a network of local colleagues who share their interests and concerns in nearly 200 ACEI state associations, provisional state affiliates and local branches.

**Career Growth**—ACEI Members enjoy special recognition resulting from their affiliation with the most active and widely recognized association in the world concerned with *both* childhood education and the professional development of educators.

**Journal of Research in Childhood Education**— Members are eligible for a special rate on the *Journal of Research in Childhood Education*, a scholarly publication bringing readers the latest results of university research in whole-child educational theory and practice. Published twice annually.

**Publications Catalog**—ACEI Members receive discounts of up to 30% on items listed in the ACEI Publications Catalog, containing dozens of resource publications and position papers.

**Discounts and Financial Services**—Travel discounts, a credit card program and group benefits such as personal and professional insurance are available to ACEI Members.

---

## ACEI Membership Application

### ☑ *Yes, please enroll me as a member of ACEI!*

| First name | MI | Last name |
|---|---|---|

Address

Address (Second line if necessary)

| City | State/Province | Zip/Postal Zone |
|---|---|---|

**Membership Category and Dues** (in US Dollars)

☐ Professional........................................................ $45
☐ Student*.............................................................. $26
☐ Retired................................................................$23

Student membership is available only to full-time students. A transcript of grades or signature of your adviser is required.
All memberships include $23.00 for subscription to *Childhood Education*.

**ACEI Division Membership** (optional)
Check Division(s) you wish to join:
☐ Division for Infancy................................................$7
☐ Division for Early Childhood............................................ $7
☐ Division for Later Childhood/Early Adolescence............. $7

**Research Journal Subscription** (special member price)
☐ One-year subscription to *Journal of Research in Childhood Education*...........................................$28

**Total Payment Enclosed:**

| | |
|---|---|
| ACEI International Dues | $ _____ |
| Division Dues | $ _____ |
| Research Journal Subscription | $ _____ |
| Foreign Members Postage | $ 10.00 |
| **TOTAL PAYMENT** | $ _____ |

**Method of Payment**

☐ Check enclosed (Payable to ACEI)
☐ VISA     ☐ Mastercard

| Card number | Expires |
|---|---|
| Signature | MC Interbank # |

Send completed forms to:
**Association for Childhood Education International**
11501 Georgia Avenue, Suite 315
Wheaton, Maryland 20902
(301) 942-2443 (800) 423-3563

DC

(facsimile accepted)